WORK

ON YOUR

GAME

WORK

ON YOUR

GAME

USE THE PRO ATHLETE MINDSET TO DOMINATE YOUR GAME IN BUSINESS, SPORTS, AND LIFE

DRE BALDWIN

New York Chicago San Francisco Athens London Madrid
Mexico City Milan New Delhi Singapore Sydney Toronto

1 2 3 4 5 6 7 8 9   LCR   24 23 22 21 20 19

ISBN   978-1-260-12137-7
MHID   1-260-12137-2

e-ISBN   978-1-260-12139-1
e-MHID   1-260-12139-9

Library of Congress Cataloging-in-Publication Data

Names: Baldwin, Dre, author.
Title: Work on your game : use the pro athlete mindset to dominate your game in business, sports, and life / Dre Baldwin.
Description: New York : McGraw-Hill, [2019] | Includes index.
Identifiers: LCCN 2018045001| ISBN 9781260121377 (alk. paper) | ISBN 1260121372
Subjects: LCSH: Success. | Sports--Psychological aspects.
Classification: LCC BF637.S8 B3265 2019 | DDC 155.4/19--dc23 LC record available at
    https://lccn.loc.gov/2018045001

McGraw-Hill Education books are available at special quantity discounts to use as premiums and sales promotions or for use in corporate training programs. To contact a representative, please visit the Contact Us pages at www.mhprofessional.com.

To Chrissindra & Derrick Baldwin
for keeping books in the house.

CONTENTS

ACKNOWLEDGMENTS

Everyone who has asked a question, offered an observation, or vented their challenges to me since 2005. *Everything is material.*

INTRODUCTION
Why Work On Your Game Exists

Anyone who knows me knows: I give it to you straight, no sugarcoating. My aim is not to make you happy, but to create success stories and help you invest in and generate results. I know how to put all the BS aside and get things done, and I'll teach you how to do the same.

Throughout this book, you'll get to know me more. You'll learn that I've been through rough stuff. I've failed, fallen flat on my face, been knocked down, counted out, and disregarded. But, I still made it happen for myself while running on my own energy.

My background is a background which everyone has heard of and seen, but less than 1 percent of the human population ever lives. And, even though my personal story is off the beaten path, I'll articulate clearly my understanding of the challenges you face, and I'll tell you exactly what you *need* to hear, not what you *want* to hear.

I originally introduced the *Work On Your Game* philosophy for athletes, from amateur to professional, to improve their mental games both inside and outside of their sports. The philosophy quickly grew outside the bounds of competitive sports and found its way into boardrooms and sales teams. *Work On Your Game* is a formula for achievement for anyone who is ready to grow and own their game, no matter what that game may be. *Work On Your Game* is a step-by-step process that maximizes you and your ability and, by definition, eliminates competition: you at your best cannot be replicated or replaced.

If all of that inspires you, you're in the right place. If this is your introduction to me, nice to meet you.

EIGHTH GRADE ADVICE

The best advice I ever received was from an eighth grader who had beaten me 10–0 in a game of one-on-one. And before you say advice from an eighth grader is too basic for you, I'm calling bullshit. It's exactly what you need, so stick around. It will be worth it, I promise.

We were riding home from our middle school pregraduation trip, and I was seated next to Brandon Abney, the best basketball player in our school. I asked Brandon for some advice on my still-weak basketball game. As the best basketball player I had direct access to, I looked up to Brandon. Anything he said about the game was something I would take and run with. And what Brandon said next changed my life forever.

"Dre, you have to do two things.

1. Stop playing scared.
2. Buy a game."

Brandon's wisdom was far beyond his 14 years.

These instructions became the foundation of not only what I did on the basketball court, but what I do in all aspects of my business and my life.

At first I didn't quite understand what Brandon meant by "buy a game."

I came to the conclusion that it simply meant "get some skills"—which meant to put in the time, work harder, and get better. Today, the phrase *Buy a Game* still means putting in the time to get the results you want. I don't care what your job is, what title you have, or where you work. No matter the circumstance, if you don't work, you'll have no game.

EXAMINE YOUR GAME

You'll see *Examine Your Game* boxes like this throughout the book. These boxes will include questions and ideas for you to think through and answer about your game, your progress, and what needs to be changed, stepped up, or eliminated.

THE START OF WORK ON YOUR GAME

I've been spreading this message since May 2005 when I started blogging on Blogspot.com. Work On Your Game (WOYG) was birthed in January 2009 when I spoke those exact words on camera at the 24 Hour Fitness gym in Cutler Bay, Miami, at two in the morning. We will get into all of that later, but first let's get back to how and why I was receiving such profound advice from a 14-year-old kid.

• • •

Julia R. Masterman Junior and Senior High, located at 17th and Spring Garden Streets in Philadelphia, was my school from the fifth through eighth grade.

While I left Masterman after the eighth grade, Brandon, who'd given me the "stop playing scared" and "buy a game" advice, continued at Masterman where he played four years of varsity basketball. I, conversely, would be attending George Washington Carver High School of Engineering and Science, or E&S, where I would . . . well, I didn't really know. I was bragging to everyone who would listen, though, that I was going to make the varsity basketball team at E&S as a freshman.

Before going our separate ways from middle school, Brandon graciously pointed out some of my playing deficiencies. He knew my abilities from the lunchtime pickup games on Masterman's rooftop playground. He could tell that I always played as if I were nervous or scared.

He was right. I *was* both nervous and scared, mostly because I had no game. I was nervous about messing up and letting my much-better teammates down (which I ended up doing anyway). I was nervous about having the ball and not knowing what to do with it (this happened too many times to count). And, I was afraid of shooting an airball or missing a layup in front of all the girls who were watching (which is exactly what happened anyway).

Brandon explained that if I was going to become a competent basketball player, I had to play fearlessly. I couldn't hesitate or be worried about messing up. In order to erase that fear, I needed to hone my skills, which would naturally expand my confidence.

At age 14, I couldn't dribble a basketball very well and I was an unreliable outside shooter. I had only a loose understanding of the concept of defense. I didn't like being thrown hard bullet passes, because I couldn't catch. I had the desire to be a useful player, but I just did not have the skills. And at 14, I didn't know "skills" went further than dribbling, passing, and shooting. Skills also included Confidence, Discipline, Mental Toughness, and Personal Initiative.

EXAMINE YOUR GAME

When is the last time you took voluntary
action to get better at your job?

My challenge as a teenager, knowing that I lacked *game*, was figuring out exactly how I could improve my game. What were the specific actions I needed to take? I knew that my current skill level wasn't enough to be taken seriously as a player, and I knew my mental game—playing tentatively, indecisively, and generally lacking confidence—needed improvement. I had to figure out all the steps to close the gap between where I was and where I wanted to be.

It's been more than 20 years since that bus ride, and I've come to learn that Brandon's advice was absolutely right: Skills + Mental Game = Success.

WORKING ON MY OWN GAME

Following Brandon's advice, I felt I had bought a healthy amount of game by my eleventh grade year—but I was cut from my high school's varsity basketball team, again, on the first day of tryouts. By this point, I knew I had the skills; the missing piece was getting my mental game in the right space. At that time, I lacked the confidence to display all my abilities under the pressure of the moment. I developed just enough confidence to finally make the team as a senior (where I sat the bench all season).

As a college player, my poor practice habits got me kicked off the team as a junior. Nothing came easy for me after that. My first two jobs after college, before my professional athletic career took off, were at Foot Locker and Bally Total Fitness.

When transitioning from professional athlete to business-person, I applied the same techniques that I'll share throughout this book. I share my philosophy so that you too can not only reach the top of your game, but stay there.

Your Game

I stopped playing professional basketball in 2015. People often ask what provoked me to leave the game, especially since I was still in pretty good shape, worked out every day, and had not suffered any major injuries. Maybe you've wondered why *any* professional athlete would walk away from the game, other than old age or injury. Is it that we grow tired of the screaming fans and relatively light work hours, all while earning a decent pay-check? Of course not—that's the fun part. Most people would not walk away from that very easily. For me, and the myriad for-mer pros I've asked this same question, it was the daily grind that pushes you out: the training, recovery, and preparation required to remain at that peak level, mentally and physically. That part of the process was what I was done with (and still do not miss). I never grew tired of the games or the fans or the attention. I just no longer wanted to make the physical and mental investments that started the chain of events that led to the trappings of a professional athlete's life.

This situation doesn't only happen in sports—it happens in boardrooms, new businesses, and everywhere else. No matter your industry or experience level, when you no longer want to work on your game, the game is over.

Unfortunately, some people stay in the game far past the point where they've stopped working.

Every game has winners and losers. It has been said that the toughest games reveal our character. Those who want to believe that winning and losing don't matter are those who usually lose. The purpose of *Working On Your Game* is to win: to prepare, perform, produce a result, and enjoy the spoils of victory. This process can and will be tough, and it will challenge you. But when you become, do, and have what you want, the payoff is more than worth all of the hard work and sacrifice that went into it.

Notice that I didn't say the game had to be fun at all times. You don't need to be excited nor motivated to show up, compete, and do your job. The only thing you need to win, in any game, is the mental tools that unlock the physical tools that allow you to prepare and perform at your best.

Some sports leagues outside of the United States utilize a system of *relegation*, in which the worst-performing teams in a league are demoted to a lower league, and the best teams from that lower league, conversely, are promoted. The business world has a similar system, where those who underperform or remain stagnant for long enough find themselves out of the game.

──────────── EXAMINE YOUR GAME ────────────

What are you consistently doing to progress in your game?

THE FOUR
WORK ON YOUR GAME PRINCIPLES

As a philosophy, *Work On Your Game* is based on four results—driven principles that apply across all professions, tasks, and hobbies for any person of any age:

1. **Discipline:** Showing up day after day to do the work.
2. **Confidence:** Putting yourself out there, boldly and authentically, to be seen, heard, and judged.
3. **Mental Toughness:** Continuing to be disciplined and confident, even when doing so hasn't yet produced the results you expected.
4. **Personal Initiative:** The capacity to take chances, bet on yourself, seize and create opportunities, and make things happen, rather than waiting for things to happen.

Look at any work you've done, professionally or personally, paid or not, where you have produced results and felt you achieved some level of success: the *Work On Your Game* principles have been part of your success.

MAKE *WORK ON YOUR GAME* YOUR OWN

Whenever I read books like the one you're reading now, I would always unconsciously wonder to myself, *How am I gonna remember and actually use all of this?* The answer is to internalize what you learn.

Internalizing is deeper than memorizing or remembering something. Internalizing means making new knowledge a part of your being through repeated application. Repetition—such as reading this book over and over again—can help with memorization, but repetition alone isn't enough to derive real value from information. It's the *use* of the information that makes it real for you. That's the commitment I want you to make with this book.

• • •

I played college basketball at Penn State Altoona, an NCAA Division 3 (D3) school. Honestly, most D3 athletes know that their college years mark the end of their athletic careers. Among my teammates at Altoona, my athletic ability alone made me stand out, even when I was playing at half-speed. This fooled me into thinking things would always be that way.

One day, a couple of college teammates and I went to play pickup basketball at St. Francis University, a Division 1 (D1) school in nearby Loretto, Pennsylvania. If you've ever watched pro basketball on TV, almost all of those players come from D1 programs, schools like St. Francis. These are the players at the top of the food chain, on full-ride scholarships in exchange for their athletic talents. D3 schools don't even offer athletic scholarships.

On this day, one particular play at St. Francis served as a major wake-up call for me.

I was swooping toward the basket on a breakaway, ball cupped in my right arm, poised to throw down a tomahawk dunk. The only person on the court who had a chance to get between me and the basket was a six-foot-seven-inch St. Francis player named Chris. I was the most athletic player at Altoona, and Chris was the same in Loretto.

I jumped. Chris *jumped*. We met in the air, the ball 11 feet above the floor (the basket is 10 feet high), 3 feet to the right of the rim. The next thing I remember is lying on the floor face up. Chris had easily blocked my dunk and taken the ball out of my hand in midair. He was standing next to my supine body, still holding the ball. The sudden halt of my momentum had sent me crashing to the floor, and everyone had gathered around to make sure I was OK. While I was a bit physically shaken from falling so hard, it was my bruised ego that needed the ice pack.

Riding back to Altoona after the games that night, I realized a few things.

One, the skills that I'd thought would be my meal ticket to pro basketball weren't even an appetizer to these D1 guys. Two, when playing against the best players, like those at St. Francis, I couldn't coast through games as I'd conditioned myself to do against the weaker competition at Altoona. The mental aspect of my game couldn't be a luxury; it was a requirement. Three, this had happened in the spring semester of my senior year. The players I would face at the pro level would be just as talented as the guy who'd blocked my dunk attempt. I needed to get my stuff together, and I needed to hurry up.

In sports, especially basketball, fewer than 1 percent of players become pros—and at the pro level, everyone has physical ability. (Similarly, at the professional level of business, everyone has knowledge, education, and experience.) Once you're in the pros, skills—including knowledge and physical game—are a commodity. While you surely *need* skill to get there, skill *alone* won't keep you there.

Well, if everyone at the top level has skills, you may be wondering, what is the difference between the All-Stars and the benchwarmers? The CEOs and those stuck in middle management? What makes one a legend, while others never move past "potential"?

The difference is the *mental game*.

At every level (playground, high school, college, and pro), I played with and against players who had more athletic talent than I did (they were taller, ran faster, and jumped higher), who never made it beyond a certain level. Some didn't have the confidence to show all of their game when called on. Many lacked the discipline to focus on their game while leaving everything else (drugs, alcohol, woman chasing, the streets) alone. Several didn't have the mental toughness to stick to a program and keep working when the expected results were late to show.

If every basketball player understood and applied the Work On Your Game principles, I would not have become a professional athlete, because there were too many players out there with even more talent than I had. Though I was blessed with some God-given ability, I made up in mental game what I lacked in talent. It's what I still do now—and what you will learn to do too.

You cannot afford a deficiency in the mental game. When you're a pro, competing against the best, there is no room to feel sorry for yourself. You must have full belief in your game, even if the next guy is objectively better than you (for now). Even when you're unsure of your skills, you can't show it. Anything you lack can and will be used against you, and the grim reality is, unlike for me that day at St. Francis, no one gathers around to check on you when you fall down.

YOU WANT TO BE A *WHAT*?

After graduating from Penn State Altoona in 2004 with a business management and marketing degree, I moved back to my parents' home in Philadelphia. It wasn't more than 48 hours before Mom wanted to have what became "The Conversation."

There I was in my parents' bedroom, Mom asking me what my future plans were, now that I'd graduated.

At that point, my hoops ambition was nothing more than a dream, but I wasn't yet ready to be "realistic." So I told my parents that I was going to become a professional basketball player.

Mom stopped folding her clothes and gave me a wide-eyed stare. Dad, who had been half-facing me, turned his body to see me directly.

"You want to be a *what?*" Mom asked, as more of a demand than a question.

"I'm going to play basketball," I replied sheepishly.

"Where?" she asked, half confused and half annoyed.

I answered honestly. "I don't know yet."

From there, Mom went on a three-minute tirade that summarized the 22-year vision she'd had for her children. She had sacrificed a lot of time and energy to make sure my sister Latoya and I both got the best education. And it was important to her that we finish school and acquire good, acceptable, and secure jobs.

Latoya, a high-achieving academic, had lived out Mom's plan. Latoya had earned multiple degrees from University Of Pennsylvania and Stanford. I had executed a solid 95 percent of the plan, but, in my one statement about playing basketball professionally, I was going to throw away all my mother's sacrifices for a pipe dream. That was her perspective, at least.

To Mom, my hoop dream was a personal affront to her 22 years of struggle and strife, money-saving and bill-paying. For the first and only time in this conversation, Mom addressed basketball directly.

"If you wanna play basketball, join a men's league or something!" she declared.

Dad didn't say much, but he did offer two pieces of feedback:

1. He told me that I could go on websites like Career-Builder.com to aid my job search. To this day, I hate CareerBuilder.com.

2. He shared with me that when Latoya and I were younger, he'd had an opportunity to travel and tour as a

musician. He turned it down because his full-time day job wouldn't have granted the time off, and he couldn't afford to leave that job with a wife and two young children to support.

I wasn't sure what to make of this second point. Was he telling me that secure, steady work was more important than doing what I really wanted to do? Was he telling me it wasn't possible to both do what I wanted in life *and* pay my bills doing it?

The whole conversation, if you want to call it that, didn't last very long. Everything Mom and Dad had said was logical, reasonable, and true. No intelligent person would have considered my basketball "plan" a sound one. So, being broke, jobless, and without any moneymaking prospects in basketball or otherwise, I went in my bedroom and cried. Not because I was sad, and not because I was disappointed my parents wouldn't support my dreams. I cried because I was angry that the truth was the truth. I was angry that I was being told it was time to be "realistic." I was angry that after four years of college, I was face-to-face with the real world, and I didn't like what I was seeing.

While I believed I still could become everything I had always seen myself becoming (well-known, rich, and idolized by fans), that wasn't what kept my desire burning. Instead it was my determination to prove that I absolutely would not, under any circumstances, let them (parents, past coaches, rival players, college professors, and peers) win.

Call that mentality what you want. All that matters is that it worked for me.

When I cried that day in 2004, I was at an emotional peak. You know, one of those rare life experiences when you never forget what happened in that moment, where you were, and who was involved. Things that happen while at an emotional peak get burned into our subconscious in such a way that it shapes and drives our behavior long after the peak moment has passed. These moments shape our lives and who we become as people. The moment I've described is the reason everything that happened after, happened.

And those tears that came from my emotional peak that day are the reason I became a professional athlete and, by extension, the only reason you're holding this book in your hands.

That was the last time I cried, because it was the last time I felt completely powerless to make things happen in my own life. Those tears guaranteed that I would never feel that way again.

And I never have.

WHO DO YOU PLAY FOR?

When playing or practicing basketball, I'd always wondered if I looked as good to an observer as I thought I looked in my own mind. Sometimes I'd do something while practicing alone that I wished I had proof of. I had a few dunks in my college career that I know were certified highlights—except that there were no cameras in the gym and no one who wasn't there that day would ever see them. So, when I finally had footage of myself playing basketball and playing well, I needed to preserve it and keep it somewhere safe and sound.

A year after graduating college, I made plans to attend my first pro basketball exposure camp. What's an exposure camp, you ask? Imagine a job fair for athletes, but instead of shaking hands and passing out résumés, we bring our playing gear and compete in games in front of our potential future coaches and bosses.

I signed up for a camp called Infosport that was being held in Altamonte Springs, Florida. My two college teammates and

I drove from Philadelphia the night before the start of camp. I played well at the camp, received a glowing scouting report, and even had all my games video recorded. I finally had proof of my basketball skill with this footage, footage that would serve as proof to pro basketball decision makers that I was good enough to play at the highest level of the game.

My performance at Infosport jump-started my career. I signed with my first agent that summer, and quickly after, I landed a job playing in Kaunas, Lithuania. After that I played for a traveling team in the United States and then in Mexico, all within two years of graduating college. My hoop dream was actually happening, and it all started from having proof of my ability to perform.

The only issue was, this proof was on a VHS tape.

If you aren't familiar with VHS, just know it's a physical copy of a recording, which meant the content couldn't be viewed unless it was in your physical possession. But luckily, at the time, digital online video was becoming popular.

I got this particular VHS footage transferred to a CD, put that CD in the drive of a desktop computer, and published my first basketball video on April 28, 2006, to a brand-new site called YouTube. I uploaded the video not to get attention, but strictly for safekeeping purposes. I was not a known athlete at the time and had never even been on TV. I wasn't expecting anyone to watch a Dre Baldwin video, much less be looking for one.

And I was right. No one was looking for *me*, but many people were looking for help with their basketball skills.

Publishing free training guides, for basketball or any other sport, did not exist in 2006. I didn't recognize this as an opportunity until months later, when I logged onto YouTube just to make sure my video was still there. What I saw shocked me.

There were *comments.*

Real, human people had watched my three-minute high-light tape and had left comments and questions:

Who do you play for?
What school did you go to?
Who taught you how to play?
Have you ever tried out for the NBA?
What's your vertical jump measurement?
How often do you practice?
*Can you make more videos on _____ (shooting/
dribbling/jumping/defense)?*

I was excited. All the questions being asked were things I actually *could* do and/or explain. I just needed to get them all on video. I started to bring my new $100 digital camera with me to the gym every day to film myself. Between 2006 and 2009, I created a brand-new genre of sharing basketball videos for others to learn from, which is now a full-fledged business for thousands of people worldwide.

Early on, my publishing on YouTube was very sporadic. Despite that, my small-but-growing band of followers wanted to know more about the random basketball guy on that new You-Tube site. As I published more drills and tips, viewers began asking about my playing mindset. They asked questions such as:

- *How did you remain confident while getting cut three years in a row from your high school varsity?*
- *What keeps you coming to the gym every day when you (sometimes) don't even have a playing contract?*
- *I really appreciate you sharing this stuff. I'm 27 and people have been telling me it's too late to go after my basketball*

dreams. Seeing you out there every day has made me believe I can do it too. Thank you!

- *We understand your motivation to sign a contract and play pro. But what's your motivation to put all this stuff on You-Tube? What do you get out of it?*

While addressing these questions, I started talking about the way I approached the game and my life, which was rooted in Mental Toughness, Confidence, and Discipline. On Monday, October 4, 2010, my Weekly Motivation series began, where I discussed a topic that applied not only to sports but to life. This series led to me writing my books *The Mental Handbook* and *The Mirror of Motivation*.

When I decided to stop playing basketball in 2015, I had positively influenced the lives of millions of people, both athletes and nonathletes, online. Today I share what I learned from my experiences through activities such as consulting, podcasting, speaking, and writing. And that's where the spaces of my life and career came together to create the book that you are holding in your hands right now.

Work On Your Game is not about making you into a professional athlete, speaker, podcaster, or preparing you for any other specific job. Instead, *Work On Your Game* will push you to maximize your potential so you can become, do, and achieve whatever you want—and there *is* something you want.

WHAT YOU'RE GETTING

Work On Your Game is about the mindset I taught myself while creating my basketball career, my personal brand, and my business. The most important skill you'll learn in this book is how to be a true professional, no matter your line of work. Being a professional is not about contracts, titles, or money. A business suit doesn't make you a professional any more than a pair of Jordan sneakers would make you a basketball player. It is about being the person who shows up and gets the job done every time, regardless of what you're feeling inside.

This book is not made to make you feel good for a while and then collect dust on a shelf. The goal of *Work On Your Game* is the same as it has been in all of my videos, blogs, books, live streams, podcasts, and interviews since 2005: to change lives.

You will maximize your game, whatever it is, and squeeze all the juice out of your opportunities, as long as you agree to the following four ideas.

1. **The mental game controls every other game.** Mastering your mental game makes every other game "work."
2. If you read and enjoy this book, then put it on a shelf and do nothing with what you have learned, it's not the fault of me nor the book. That is your fault. **You must put in the work and apply what you learn.**
3. If you **take in, follow, and apply what I give you** in *Work On Your Game*, you will be playing the mental game at a new level, the level of someone who makes it to the top 1 percent in his or her chosen profession.
4. How much you believe this book will help you plays a big part in if and how much it actually helps you. So, **what you believe and expect is usually what you get.**

• • •

When you're ready to shift your life to a whole new level, turn the page and let's work on your game.

WORK
ON YOUR
GAME

1

CARDIO FOR THE MIND

Physical conditioning is a key aspect of athletic training, and mental conditioning unlocks your physical tools. Your brain is a muscle that needs daily exercise to remain sharp and strong, just as your body does.

In basketball, which is a game of running more than it is a game of shooting or dribbling, proper conditioning is a necessary-but-hated aspect of game preparation. Basketball conditioning exercises range from full-court wind sprints to running hills to flipping industrial-sized tires, and I'm sure there's new stuff that even I haven't heard about yet.

One drill I am sure all players are familiar with is the "suicide" (or "running lines"). The drill is simple. You start on the baseline (the out-of-bounds space behind the basket). You sprint from the baseline to four different points on the court: first, one-quarter of the way and back (to the foul line extended); second, halfway and back (to half-court), third, three-quarters of the way and back (the opposite foul line), and fourth the full length of the court and back.

Your legs fatigue doing the suicide, but your burning lungs and shortness of breath are most responsible for the discomfort.

Aside from the cardiovascular benefit, basketball coaches use suicides as punishment for myriad player infractions. While running a suicide, the basketball court becomes much longer than it looks on TV. Conditioning your mind, while usually not physically uncomfortable, also requires grit and endurance.

In this chapter, you'll learn how to condition your mind to be more than ready for the challenges you'll face in the game of life.

THE TRUMPET OF VICTORY

If you think of legendary war generals whose names you know, you may consider Napoleon Bonaparte. Hannibal. Julius Caesar. And Alexander the Great.

Alexander never shied away from battle. However, in one particular engagement, Alexander's army wasn't faring well. Known to fight alongside his troops, Alexander surveyed the battlefield and decided it would be smarter to retreat and live to fight another day, rather than suffer mass casualties. Alexander signaled to the rear of the army to his trumpet boy, who would play the "trumpet of retreat," alerting the soldiers to disengage and exit.

Alexander continued to fight, but a few minutes passed and no trumpet sounded. Alexander gave the signal again, and still no trumpet. This was a matter of literal life and death. Alexander went to the rear himself now, demanding the trumpet boy be brought before him. The trumpet boy sheepishly explained that, because he had grown so accustomed to the army *winning* battles, he no longer carried the trumpet of retreat with him.

The battle was still going on, and Alexander's army was still losing, so Alexander had to think quickly.

He got an idea: If all we have is the Trumpet of Victory, then play the Trumpet of Victory.

What happened next?

The Trumpet of Victory was sounded, and Alexander's army, once facing sure defeat, rallied back to win the battle.

It's important to think about the mental conditioning of Alexander's army in their response to the trumpet. Even though the individual soldiers couldn't see the entire battlefield, the entire army was conditioned to know that the Trumpet of Victory meant they could finish off the enemy if each soldier gave his all for one final push.

So, how does this relate to you at work?

Think of your last hour of the day, your last set in the gym, or your last class of school for the day. You're fatigued and depleted, but knowing that there's only *one more* left—one more phone call, one more meeting, one more assignment, one more drill—we somehow always find the energy to push ourselves when we can see a finish line that's not far away. So you know you can condition yourself, at least temporarily, to "bring it" and give your best effort when you want or need to. The purpose of conditioning yourself mentally is to bring this energy level as a normal, everyday way of being.

Play *Your Own* Trumpet

What's your Trumpet of Victory? What idea, thought, or signal do you give yourself in order to give your best push and finish what you started? Do you have a routine or process for playing your trumpet?

No matter your answer, let's dive into how to create a signal and routine:

1. **Choose your signal.** What signal will tell you it's time to give your best? Your cues should be 100 percent under your control so you can play your trumpet any time it's needed. As an athlete, I wore a short-sleeve T-shirt over my game jersey during warm-ups; taking off that T-shirt was my signal that it was Showtime.

2. **Develop your routine.** Think of your routine as setting up the cameras, lighting, and microphones on a stage before a play or a concert. When the spotlight shines and the curtain opens, your Trumpet of Victory needs to be playing. Your routine is the runway for your Trumpet of Victory. As a basketball player, I had a specific dynamic warm-up routine: High knees. Heel kicks. Dynamic stretch of both movements. Hip swings. Dynamic hamstring stretch. Calf stretch. This got my body ready to go, and, since it was a routine I didn't need to think about consciously, I could focus my mind on my upcoming performance.

3. **Do your homework.** A singer has sound check; a salesperson practices her presentation; an actor has dress rehearsal—all so that when performance time arrives, their minds are in game mode. As a player, I maintained a strict ten-to-one practice-to-game ratio at minimum: I would work on my game, practicing alone at least ten times for every one game I played in (including half-court one-on-one and pickup games, not just official games with my teams).

On the opposite end of the spectrum, there are also Negative Trumpets that you should make sure you are *not* sounding.

These may be unconsciously playing on their own because you aren't fully aware of them—and they must be silenced. These Negative Trumpets may include:

- Quitting
- Second-guessing yourself
- Laziness
- Feeling sorry for yourself

As you start to be more aware of these Negative Trumpets, ask yourself: What situations trigger them to play in your mind?

● ● ●

Alexander's army was conditioned to finish off a rival army when the signal sounded, regardless of what was happening before the signal. For you to hear *your* Trumpet of Victory, you must eliminate these unproductive trumpets and clear your mind of any mental triggers that lead to these trumpets playing.

ANT EXTERMINATION

I can tell you from experience: having ants in your home is not fun.

They are small enough to fit into anything that isn't sealed airtight. And if you can see one, you can bet that there are countless others. A thorough housecleaning or good exterminator eliminates ants, but you're the one who has to make sure there's nothing in your home that brings them back.

Our minds have their own ANTs—*automatic negative thoughts*. These ANTs can live for years, subsisting on your thoughts as food. Mental ANTs know your brain's terrain even better than you know it, and they aren't easily disposed of.

Do you know someone who always finds a way to get upset, no matter what is happening? What about the person who, when presented with a possibility, immediately thinks of all the possible pitfalls and reasons it would *not* work? These are just two of many ways ANTs can show themselves.

ANTs find their way into your subconscious mind through your repetitive thoughts. Your thoughts are affected by things such as who and what you listen to, where you spend your time, and the material you read and watch. ANTs become part of your vocabulary by habit, and they remain there unless you consciously exterminate them. Here's the three-step plan to get rid of them.

Step #1: Recognize When ANTs Come Around

The first step to killing your ANTs and keeping them away forever is becoming aware of your habits of thought. According to Dr. Bruce Lipton, former professor of medicine at Stanford University, at least 85 percent of our daily thoughts are both habitual and unconscious. This means we don't actually control most of our thoughts, and we are unaware that the thoughts are even occurring.

And, just like with real ants, you have to catch them where they live. Notice yourself reacting negatively to a situation, and question where that energy is coming from. The answers you get help you find the nest your ANTs live in.

Step #2: Have ANTs? Don't Beat Yourself Up Over It!

When you find ANTs (and you will, because everyone has at least a few), be appreciative of the fact that you now have the skills to identify them. Most people never even know they have them. At least now you can do something about them.

Step #3: Exterminate the ANTs

If you notice any negative thoughts, immediately cancel them out with at least two positive thoughts on the situation at hand. By reversing that negative conditioning, you are turning your mind around in the direction you want it to go.

WHO'S THE BOSS?

As I mentioned previously, 85 percent of our thoughts are habitual. Our words and actions follow the same pattern. Human life in general is based around habits, from the side of the bed we sleep on, to our driving routes, to our body language. If there's any area of our life in which we feel we need improvement, we must start with our *habits* in that area.

According to the *New Oxford American Dictionary*, a *habit* is "a settled or regular tendency or practice, especially one that is hard to give up." Habits take a load off your mind the same way a personal assistant takes work off your hands. Each habit you form equals one less thing to think about because your reaction happens unconsciously. In this way, habits are useful: we don't have to decide each day which route to take to work or how to tie our shoes. But not all habits are helpful. We also develop unproductive habits, and people have a tendency to believe their unproductive habits are out of their control. In these cases, you'll hear phrases such as, "That's just who I am" or "I can't help it." Believing that your habits control you is a surefire way to remain the same.

For example, I grew up with a habit of eating candy, and lots of it. Skittles, Nerds, Mike and Ikes—anything that was colorful and fruity—as well as Sugar Babies. This particular bad habit definitely achieved a result, a result that I didn't want: I had to get six cavities filled when I was 16 years old. The candy-eating habit surely "worked": against me and my teeth.

One day a live stream video commentator asked me how I developed the ability to talk calmly and steadily without notes or pausing to think of what to say next. I replied that it was my habit of doing videos, live streams, podcasts, and written content that conditioned me for thinking on my feet. I could formulate and speak on a topic without "pregame" preparation. Though this talk-without-stopping skill wasn't why I started sharing content online, the habit produced a result nonetheless.

You see, your whole life is a reflection of your habits. If you and I stood together on a corner in Miami Beach and watched people walk by, we could guess, relatively accurately, each person's exercise and nutrition habits just by looking at their bodies: those habits don't hide.

People come to know us, and we come to know ourselves, by our most consistent actions or habits. The things you do consistently, with your body, mind, time, money, energy, and everything else, become who you are. Your unique combination of habits becomes your character, and your character points you to your destiny.

▬▬▬ YOUR HABITS CAN WORK FOR YOU ▬▬▬

If you've ever sat in an employee review meeting, you know what happens: your work performance is on trial. Your boss praises what you do well, and tells you what you could do better. Not every employee still has a job at the end of review day, but that's part of the game.

When it comes to your habits, you are the boss, owner, supervisor, *and* HR manager all at the same time. And reviews should happen much more often than they do in the business world.

Instead of every 6 or 12 months, you should review each of your habits daily. When you conduct this daily review, notice your settled and regular tendencies and ask yourself review questions such as *Is this habit helping me? Is it making me better? Is it taking me where I want to be?*

If the answer is yes, congratulations! You have a habit that is taking you where you want to go.

If no, you have two options:

1. **If the habit is salvageable, decide what adjustments need to be made.** For example, when situations go "off-script" in life, you probably react some way mentally. So, instead of asking, *Why is this always happening to me?* change the question to, *Where's the opportunity in this?* You'll see the habit of asking a question is still there, but it's been adjusted to be positive.

   A basketball player who is bad at shooting three-point shots may be better served in the long term by making some adjustments to his shooting technique, versus giving up ever trying to shoot a three-point shot again. If the habit is fixable, make an adjustment.

2. **Fire the habit and replace it with a new, more productive one right away.** What habit can go in this place that will actually serve you instead of hurting you? For example, a recovering alcoholic is advised to not go to the places that previously triggered the drinking and to find some new hangout spots. All the old, drinking-related habits have to go permanently.

Neither method is necessarily better than the other, but in both cases it's important to recognize what you can fix and fix it or discover what should be replaced and replace it.

Now, with positive, productive habits firmly established, and useless habits making their way out of your life, you have cleared a path to move yourself to the next level.

GET ON A NEW LEVEL

Taking your game to a new level is about more than skills. You need to create a new vision of yourself, for yourself. The old you must go away to make room for the "new and improved" you. This is accomplished in three simple steps:

Step 1. Change Your Beliefs About Who You Are

What you see in the mirror determines the life you'll live. Often what we see in the mirror is a vision others put there: parents who wanted to steer our lives in a certain direction, friends who felt they knew what was best for us, naysayers who tried to tamp down our ambitions. Just as often, we find ourselves living out the default vision modeled from the people around us.

Start changing these automatic beliefs about yourself and think about what it is you really want for yourself and your life. Then consider the question: Who do you need to become to make that real? Are you a lifelong benchwarmer, or a starter in the wrong situation? Are you the mailroom minion or a future CEO? Are you out of work with no résumé, or are you set to launch the next game-changing startup in the industry? Who you believe you are determines who you really are.

Step 2. Change Your Beliefs About Who You *Aren't*

What capabilities, results, and realities do you believe are out of reach for you? Of those, how many have you actually tried to achieve or acquire? What have you *not* tried because you consider yourself incapable for reasons both inside and outside of your control such as your gender, country of origin, family upbringing, and more? Test these beliefs, and I think you'll find you're much more capable than you thought you were and have a lot more potential than you thought you had.

Step 3. Do What the *New* You Does

With this new vision of who you are, assume the position. What would this new you do? How do you carry yourself? How do you think? What actions does the new you take? What is no longer accceptable? Become this new person, and the actions will follow the mindset and the results follow the actions. Live out your answers through all your actions.

Expect Discomfort—and Stay There

Reaching a new level in life is exciting. You'll realize capabilities that you otherwise never would have tapped into. Letting go of previously held false limitations will open up a whole new world to you.

But I want to warn you, it won't all be perfect. This new way of living will be uncomfortable.

All of us have an internal running conversation that con-stantly plays out in our minds. This conversation tells us who we are, who we're not, what we're comfortable with, and what we'd prefer to avoid. The actions, thoughts, and ideas of this new-level you are foreign objects to your long-running internal conversation. Without constant, strong reinforcement of the new-level material, your mind will reject this new mindset and everything it represents. It's uncomfortable to the old you.

This resistance toward that discomfort is the exact reason many people never grow or improve. It's not because they don't *want* to, it's because who they *have been* is so firmly entrenched in them that they can't fathom being or doing anything else. Don't let this be you. Remain vigilant and catch any "old level" thoughts that are trying to exert seniority over the new you.

ASK YOURSELF A BETTER QUESTION

In the early 2000s, Apple realized that battling with every computer company in the market was a bloody race to the bottom. Instead of asking the question everyone else was asking—*How can we sell more computers than the next guy?*—Apple asked a better question: How can we eliminate the other guys as competitors altogether? The iPod and iPhone were results of this shift in mindset.

According to the documentary series *The Defiant Ones*, music mogul Dr. Dre found himself constantly turning down endorsement offers. A company once even offered Dre a footwear line, which Dre promptly declined. As Dre lamented the many unexciting and off-brand offers he had been turning away, Dre's business partner, Jimmy Iovine, asked a better question: what if, instead of selling *sneakers*, the music legend sold *speakers*? From this better question, the Beats Electronics company, maker of popular Beats by Dr. Dre headphones, was born—and later sold to Apple for $3 billion in 2015.

When you ask a better question, you eliminate potential problems and create new opportunities. Apple's better question did exactly that, and look where the company is today.

Thinking is an internal back-and-forth question-and-answer session we have with ourselves throughout our waking hours. If you've ever seen a good lawyer in action, you know that questions can restrict and direct the answers of the person on the stand to a predetermined result. In the same way, the questions you ask in your personal Q&A are driving your thoughts and your results.

How do you ask a better question, then? First understand that our thinking is habitual. You don't consciously think about what to think most of the time; it just *happens*. So the first step in changing our thought habits is the same as the first step in changing our action habits: we must become aware of what we're doing and examine whether it's helping or not. Simple sample question: *Why am I thinking what I'm thinking?*

When you ask yourself a better question, you may realize you are trying to solve a problem that only exists because of the bad questions you've been feeding yourself. Change the question, change the answers, change the result.

THE VENDING MACHINE OF SUCCESS

We've all used vending machines before. Well, instead of snacks and candy, the Vending Machine of Success delivers your goals. Let's get familiar with the rules of the machine.

Rule #1: Pay First, Rewards Second

Countless people want results, or the promise of results, before they even start the work. But think of how a vending machine works. You put your money in first, *then* you tell the machine what you want. You trust that the machine will follow through and deliver what you paid for. And most of the time, it does.

The Vending Machine of Success works the same way. You pay first by making investments of time, energy, focus, attention, and money. You tell the machine what you want with your thoughts, words, and actions. And eventually you get what you asked for, but only when life feels you've paid the variable price—we'll get to that in Rule #4.

I know what you're thinking: "But Dre, it doesn't always work that way." You're right. So, what do you do when you feel the machine isn't working correctly? You know you've paid the price, but you still don't have what you want. Let's look at Rule #2.

Rule #2: Stuck? Shake It Up

We've all had that dreaded experience of putting money in the machine, pressing the buttons, and the potato chips you wanted so badly get stuck on the edge of that spinning coil. What do you do?

I'd probably bang on the glass of the machine (which almost never works), and if that didn't work, I'd move to the side of the machine and bang on it from there. If *that* didn't work, I would shake the vending machine (not too much), and then I'd go to my last option: find a building employee and get my money back.

Well, life is sometimes an out-of-order vending machine. You've done everything right, followed the rules, yet you still didn't see results.

The first (and most common) response is whining and complaining. Just like banging on the glass, this rarely works. I've even seen tears of sorrow, or quitting out of disgust and frustration. I've seen people watch others quit and use that as an excuse to never even try themselves.

A better option is to look at your situation like a broken vending machine and shake things up. Some ways you can do this include:

- When your phone is not ringing, start dialing numbers.
- If no one's knocking on your door, go knocking on doors.
- When you're not getting enough attention, take attention-drawing action.
- If you *are* doing the right things, do them a different way, or for a different audience, or in a different place.
- If you're doing nothing, do *something*.

These only apply if you've paid the price, because Rule #3 comes with consequences.

Rule #3: Don't Try to Cheat the Machine

Sometimes, people try to get more than they paid for and attempt to cheat the machine. Success that is obtained unethically is not real success. You didn't pay the price and didn't earn what you have. Look at the Major League Baseball players who admitted to or were found guilty of taking performance-enhancing drugs during their playing days. Even if they had stellar careers before the cheating began, many fans discredit their entire body of work because of one bad decision to cheat the vending machine.

Play the game fairly and pay the price. If you don't have the full amount to pay for what you want, save up your resources and come back for it. Whatever you get, earn it honestly.

Rule #4: Stick With It!

Walking away in frustration from a jammed machine won't get you the snack you paid for. Instead, the snack sits there, ready to go into the hands of the next persistent paying customer. Life is the same way. Remember: you don't have to walk away just because it's not working. If you really want it, commit to finding a way to get it. Never walk away from the Vending Machine of Success without getting what you've paid for, because somebody's going to get it—it might as well be you.

How many athletes quit a sport after one failed tryout? How many people hold back on improving themselves because they're worried about what others will think and say about them? How many people do you know that had the talent, resources, and opportunity to reach all of their goals, yet achieved very little? A lot.

What happens to that talent and opportunity when it's left behind? Does it:

A. Lie dormant for the rest of eternity, or

B. Go back into the universe, available to the next person who claims it?

The answer is B.

People walk away from opportunities every day. Whether as a result of frustration, fear, lack of ambition, or ignorance to the opportunity, that abandoned opportunity doesn't just disappear. Instead, it makes itself available for the next opportunistic person to claim and use.

This is how some people reach massive, seemingly unimaginable levels of success with seemingly ordinary levels of effort. They're cashing in on not only their own opportunities, but the abandoned opportunities of those who didn't stick around when things got tough. If you want to be amongst the massively successful, make the decision to hang in there and stick with it when things get tough.

Rule #5: Prices Are Subject to Change

People have asked me how I would have launched my personal brand if I were getting started today. That's a legitimate question, and a tough one. When I started building my brand with basketball videos, I created an entirely new genre. Nobody, not even the NBA itself, was putting basketball training online, and no athlete was blogging about his or her professional experience the way I was.

Now there are thousands of athletes online, on every platform, sharing everything they can think of (and things they don't think about). The space is supersaturated, and it's harder to break through now than in the early years. The price of attention now is exponentially higher than it was in 2006, and that price is going up by the day.

Is that fair? No. But, who told you it would be?

Here's the thing about the Vending Machine of Success: the prices change, often without notice.

You can't avoid this reality. What you can do is continue upping your personal value and stay ahead of the pace of inflation.

Rule #6: Press the Right Buttons to Get What You Want

I know people who are really good at what they do, and from the outside looking in things seem great. But, just because someone is great at something doesn't mean it's what he or she wants to be doing. Maybe people pursued the career that mom and dad wanted for them, or perhaps they went to the school that their teachers told them was secure. Sure, they got exactly what they were going after, but was it what they really *wanted*? Probably not.

When you put resources into achieving an outcome, make sure you're aiming for something you actually want. Be sure you are living *your* life.

The Vending Machine of Success is often unforgiving, but the process is simple to understand and apply. Put enough in, and you can have anything the machine offers.

2

THE THIRD DAY AND BEYOND

Discipline is the tool that took me from sitting at the end of my high school team's bench to signing my first professional basketball contract just five years later.

When I first started playing basketball, none of the neighborhood players could explain the process of getting better to me. These players were good, but their development had not been intentional. They just played a lot and improved by default; they couldn't teach anyone else *how* they did it. I knew that any skill could be traced back to a process, and I was determined to find that process. And, even as a teen, I knew I needed it to make this basketball thing work for me.

I was a regular at the evening pickup games at Finley Playground in my Mount Airy neighborhood in Philadelphia, but what I really needed was solo practice time. Since every player my age was already much better than I was, I couldn't just do what they did—I needed to do *more* than they were doing.

Finley's outdoor park was the only basketball court I had access to, and everyone came out to play in the evenings. However, I noticed that no one came to the basketball courts in the afternoons. And, for good reason: it was too damn hot. Who wanted to be outside, running and sweating on blacktop, when it was a humid 93 degrees? You wouldn't, and neither did I, but I had no choice. Those afternoons were the only chance I had to practice alone. And, over time, it was in these sessions that I developed the discipline and persistence that are now my most valuable talents.

Discipline and persistence became the life-changing, championship-winning formula that I applied to everything in my life.

EXAMINE YOUR GAME

Sometimes there are things that no one is doing for a good reason. Your job is to find out *why*. If the reason is discomfort, inconvenience, or general ignorance, you may have a wide-open opportunity.

KILL EXPLANATIONS AND EXCUSES

We waste a lot of our time explaining ourselves to people who may quickly try to stop us from taking action, but would just as quickly move out of our way once we've started. We share our goals with those who do nothing to help us but are quick to offer an unsolicited opinion. We're confronted by people who seem to believe that we owe them answers and explanations but are just waiting for the opportunity to throw something we said yesterday back in our faces.

None of these people, or their actions, are helping us get anywhere. But we waste valuable resources justifying ourselves to them, crafting excuses when they demand answers, and running ourselves in circles because of what we think "they" will think or say about us—resources that could be used to improve ourselves and move forward.

Use the following principles to eliminate your need for explanation and excuses, now and forever.

Stop Explaining Yourself to People

If you owe explanations to anyone, it should be a short list. Lose the need to justify your actions to anyone not directly involved in your life or work. You can't please everyone anyway, so stop trying. This point is even more important given the ubiquity of social media. Anonymous people with no faces and no names will have something to say about you and your work or life.

Don't invest your valuable time and emotional energy on others unless they're equally invested in you (and you actually want them to be). Instead, worry about making yourself better—which will benefit the people who really matter.

Your Goals Are for You Only

MMA fighter Conor McGregor once stated that announcing your goals proves that you really believe in them. Looking at his success as a fighter, you may feel this tactic worked for McGregor, but I disagree. Conor is mixing correlation (I did this, *then* this happened) with causation (this occurred *because* I did this first). Conor became a champion because of his skills, training, physical tools, know-how, experience, and self-belief. While announcing your goals may feel like a good way to hold yourself accountable, the announcement itself is not the reason you'll succeed or fail.

But it's harmless, right? Why not announce your goals to everyone?

In his 2010 TED Talk "Keep Your Goals to Yourself," Derek Sivers explains that making a public announcement of a goal creates a small amount of satisfaction in a person. Our brains don't know the difference between speaking of a *desire* versus speaking of an *accomplishment*. So, when we verbalize our goals to other people, we lose some of our drive to actually achieve them.

The only people who need to know your goals are those directly involved (or those you feel could be involved) in helping you reach them. The spectators can't help, so they don't need to know what's going on until after it happens. They'll still watch you regardless; they don't have anything else to do.

HONOR YOUR WORD

Being true to your word is the easiest way to build trust, and violating your word is the easiest way to lose it. When you set out to do something, you're giving your word to yourself. If you get it done, you learn to trust yourself more. On the opposite end of the spectrum, if you routinely violate your own trust by not doing what you told yourself you would, you'll have a hard time betting on yourself in the future.

So follow through on your word, complete your tasks, do your job every time, and you'll never need an explanation. If you sell a product, deliver what your buyers paid for. If you say you'll be somewhere, be there. If you sign a contract, honor it. If you're not sure you'll do something, don't commit to it.

When your old excuses are dead and your goals aren't public knowledge, you'll be better equipped to honor your word, go to work, and deliver.

OWN THE THIRD DAY

Even if you've never heard of the Third Day, you know it well.

Have you ever gone on a workout "vacation"? During this time period, you don't lift a weight, go for a jog, or execute a single burpee.

After this vacation ends, you return to the gym with a new trainer, new workout gear, and a new mindset about your health and fitness.

The first day is great. Sure, the workout kicks your butt and you're dead tired, but it's the first day and it's exciting and *new*. Afterward, you look in the mirror, exhale deeply, and say to yourself, *I'm DOING THIS!*

On the second day, half your body is sore, but you're driven to get back at it.

There's more new workout gear to pop the tags off of, and your sneakers still have that brand-new smell. It's only been two days, but you're starting to feel like you *belong* in the gym. You stroll in feeling like a regular. Even the friendly front desk guy remembers you from yesterday.

The second workout beats you up even worse, leaving the *other* half of your body sore. After that second workout, you drag yourself home, look in mirror, and with *slightly* less enthusiasm, say to yourself, *I'm doing this.*

On the Third Day, everything changes. Nothing feels as new and exciting anymore.

Your new sneakers feel like they're made of cement. The commute to the gym takes just a *little bit* longer. The voice of your trainer or class instructor is not as welcoming. Your body and mind are having a difference of opinion.

The Third Day, to say the least, is rough.

When Third Days Happen

Third Days are not limited to the gym or single days. You can have a Third *Week* or *Month*, and it can happen to anyone, from authors to accountants or athletes to electricians. We all have Third Days.

On the Third Day, your self-discipline reintroduces itself to you.

How we handle the Third Day when things are not new anymore, the excitement is gone, and things still need to get done is the determining factor for our long-term results.

The Third Day is about your discipline to bring your best effort, even at times when you least feel like it. Without solid discipline, you won't survive many Third Days.

Regardless of where or when it happens, every Third Day results in one of three possible outcomes:

1. The Third Day shows up, and you don't. You text your workout partner, "Hey. Not gonna make it today." *You lose.*
2. You show up, but not really. You're there, but you're not all the way *there*. You go through the motions, do the bare minimum and nothing more. *You lose.*
3. You show up, all the way. You're mentally locked in and ready to do your job. The Third Day realizes you're not going anywhere, and it gets out of your way. By sheer force of energy, you make your coworkers uncomfortable for thinking they could half-ass their workday or practice session. You who hold everyone else accountable without saying a word. *You win.*

On Third Days, you either no-show, fall into the rut of average, or find a way to fully show up, physically *and* mentally.

The key to owning the Third Day is the mental state you can get yourself into and your ability to stay there. The physical takes care of itself, as your body follows your mind. Creating this mental state is about your reasons for getting focused, so those reasons have to be important.

What You Gain from the Third Day

What do you get for having the discipline to show up on a Third Day? You get *just a little bit* ahead of everyone else who didn't show up. The amount you get ahead is so small that neither you nor the no-show sees or feels a difference. Sometimes, you may feel dumb for doing this extra work, because it seems like it's all for nothing. These extra days, hours, or minutes are the crux of the Third Day. Your relationship to the Third Day won't be obvious until it's obvious.

When I started working on my basketball game, alone and with no guidance, I was laughed at a lot. Players joked about how hard I was working in exchange for such pitiful results. These players were much better than I was, and looking at where I was with my game, they were 100 percent correct. They were pointing out the obvious, and I had no recourse.

None of us understood the Third Day back then, but, as months and years went by, my work slowly started to show itself. Every time I showed up and practiced, I was getting a tiny bit better, though, from day to day, no one could tell. Those players who were better than I was but hadn't been practicing were slowly surpassed by the players who *were* practicing. The gap between myself and those players who'd laughed at me eventually closed. And as I became more efficient in working on my game, improvements came faster and faster.

I eventually caught and moved *ahead* of the players I used to look up to—all because I beat the Third Day over and over again. The Third Day came to work for me instead of against me.

The Third Day Sees Everything

My middle school gym teacher used to say, "When you cheat or take shortcuts, the only person you're cheating is yourself." It took me years to fully understand what this meant.

When you lack discipline, the Third Day catches you from behind. The change is so subtle, though, that many don't notice it until it's too late. When you take a day off from what was a daily commitment, you think you've gotten away with it. You might think, *Maybe I can take another day off*, and you slowly create a monster.

When it comes to the Third Day, the space between cause (your Third Day efforts) and effect (the results of those efforts) is so wide that few of us ever make the connection. Conversely, many who intend to abide by the Third Day principle cannot stick to it for the exact same reason: no immediate results. Showing up consistently on the Third Day can feel (and look like) a huge waste of time. But, I guarantee you it's not—and that will become clear if you have the patience and discipline to stick around.

Working as a membership salesperson at Bally Total Fitness in 2005, I was at the facility every day because most of my paycheck was commission-based. Even if I wasn't scheduled to work, I would still schedule appointments with gym prospects.

Because I was there so much, I was very visible to gym members. When members of the gym had a problem, whether with a machine or with their membership, I started to become the person they went to. And when those same members had a friend who wanted to join, who do you think they sought out?

The commission from those sales provided the money I needed to attend that first pro basketball exposure camp that started my career. Those extra hours established my reputation for dependability, which I leveraged to get a weekend off to travel to Orlando for that life-changing camp.

TUNE OUT THE NOISE

You like the idea of the Third Day, but you're stuck being around people who aren't into the whole *discipline* thing. These can be family members, coworkers, or teammates. You're connected to them in some way that means you can't detach from them easily. So, how do you stick to your commitments, even when their negativity or lack of discipline is a constant in your environment?

I'll tell you how: don't listen.

Hearing is automatic. If I shout your name from across the street and you hear me, you'll look to see who said your name. If a loud sound happens while you're sleeping, you'll likely wake up.

While hearing is automatic, *listening* is a choice. If I speak in a quiet voice about something you deem important, you'll focus on me and listen closely to what I'm saying so you don't miss a word.

You will *hear* a lot of nonsense from losers when you're working your Third Days. Be wise enough to not *listen* to it.

Block out their negativity, and you'll be able to handle the Third Day better. String together enough Third Days over six weeks, five months, or ten years, and you'll create separation from everyone else. Just remember: this gap between you and the slackers won't be obvious until it's obvious.

While the ending sounds great, the process won't always be so enjoyable. I'll tell you right now what to expect:

You WILL question yourself.

You WILL question your plan.

You WILL wonder if you're wasting your time.

You WILL be tempted to believe that you, indeed, *are* wasting your time.

You WILL be told to give it up.

The facts WILL be thrown in your face.

You WILL try things and fail.

You WILL invest time and see no results.

You WILL feel like a dumbass, and you may even be called one.

You WILL feel like agreeing with it at times.

You WILL wake up on a Third Day, knowing what you have to do, and not want to do it.

You WILL be tempted, at times, to sleep in, take a day off, half-ass, or quit.

The decisions you make when any of the above happen—and they will—WILL make or break you.

Now, show up and give it your all on the Third Day.

DON'T STOP TRYING

There's a story behind how Formula 409, the popular all-purpose household cleaner, got its name.

According to Formula 409's website, the name is a tribute to the tenacity of the two scientists who invented it. The scientists were determined to create the greatest grease-cutting, dirt-blistering, bacteria-eliminating cleaner on the planet. It wasn't until batch number 409 that the scientists were finally satisfied with what they had, so the name stuck.

What would you try 400-plus times until you got it right?

What would make a person disciplined enough to do this or even think this way? Is it upbringing? Environment? The type of work you do? Force of circumstance?

It's none of those.

The key to discipline is wanting something strongly enough that you're willing to follow a process and delay gratification to get it.

Great business leaders inspire their teams by painting a picture of the future, and a vision of success, that everyone can see and is willing to stick to the disciplines to get to.

In your life, there are some activities and disciplines that you will always find a way to show up for and get done. I love working out; even as an ex-professional now I still make time for exercises every day. And there are things you know you *should* do that you can easily find an excuse not to—for example, I've never been keen on household cleaning. The determining factor behind both is the same: you are moved to action or inaction.

What do you want strongly enough that you're willing to be disciplined to get it? How disciplined are you capable of being? Are you willing to be disciplined for long enough to produce the outcomes you want? Are you willing to apply what you're learning to see it through to results?

If so, build your discipline by abiding by the following principles.

Master the Skill of Showing Up

Aside from aesthetics or the smoothness of the ride, many automobile manufacturers tout one specific characteristic: dependability.

The dependable car lasts hundreds of thousands of miles, has repeat buyers, and has earned a reputation that goes back decades. While some manufacturers sell luxury, prestige, and status, many consumers are concerned with safety and reliability. In other words, people want the car they can depend on to show up.

If you're a supervisor or business owner, which team members do you value the most? Those who are most consistent and reliable. The people you can depend on to show up, even if they're not the prettiest or most talented. You value their reliability because we place value in what we can predict and depend on.

Discipline is a constant, and showing up to do the work is a rare skill in itself. Consistent performance begets predictable results. This is why we have routines for the tasks most important to us. The most decorated airline pilot still follows his or her preflight checklist routine before taking off. A seasoned surgeon follows a routine before operating.

You do not obtain consistent results with randomly applied disciplines. So, be predictable.

Success and winning are all rooted in sticking to the disciplines—doing the same stuff, over and over again. In basketball, I shot the same shots and practiced the same moves thousands of times for every *one* time I did them in games. If you exercise consistently, you probably go through the same warm-up routine every time. A salesperson or public speaker has standard presentations that she has practiced and presented hundreds of times, and knows exactly how and when an audience will respond. Dunkin' Donuts' brand reputation is built on the trust that, at 5 a.m. every morning, the doughnuts are hot and the coffee is brewing.

BE PREPARED

In the animal kingdom, disciplined animals work throughout the summer and fall to gather, store, or eat heavy amounts of food to sustain themselves all winter. The animals that are prepared survive winter to see the new life of spring. In the human world, your discipline on the wintry Third Days gets you to the spring of your career and of your life. And just like in nature, your "spring" is when new opportunities are born.

Those who see discipline as boring are usually the people who most need it. To some, the very act of discipline is like living through a cold, never-ending winter. There's nothing new or exciting to do. It's the same routines every day, with no fanfare or reward. Correct me if I'm wrong, but people who see discipline this way usually have very little of it. They sit out the Third Days, longing for the fun of summer. Unfortunately, these people don't often make it to the summers.

The hardest part of discipline is the monotony: doing the same stuff over and over again, often for an extended or (seemingly) never-ending period of time. The "professional" part of being a professional athlete is not the number of games played, it's the repetitive work you do *in between* the games that's is not captured on camera that counts.

Abiding by the Third Day principle, you may not receive much tangible feedback to tell you whether you're doing the right thing or not. It's frustrating seeing others who you know haven't put in the work that you have but are enjoying the results you thought you'd be seeing. When this happens, stick to what you're doing. You *are* doing the right thing. You *are* in the right place. You *have* the right plan. You *are* the right person. Discipline is consistency and persistence of effort. You have the correct formula; just continue applying it.

SUCCESS IS NOT ON YOUR SCHEDULE

Success must have its way, or no way at all. Success doesn't care about your schedule, your feelings, or the problems in your life. Success doesn't care whether you want to work today or not. Success wants all you've got, even when you don't have much to give anymore. Success must be constantly tended to, or it will move on.

People make the mistake of treating success disrespectfully and wonder why it goes away. Those who don't respect it have likely made at least one of the following errors:

- **Belittled success.** *I'm selling my product, but have only made three sales.*
- **Didn't appreciate the little things.** *All the years I put into earning my degree, and the only job isn't even enough to pay off my loans!*
- **Failed to build on a small success.** *The coach told me I could be a team manager this year, and play on the team next year. I'm better than that, so I turned down his offer.*
- **Compared their success to someone else's.** *I was doing OK, I guess, but then I saw Lisa. Compared to her, I've done nothing!*
- **Grew impatient with success.** *I worked on my game, went to conferences and hired a coach, yet I still don't have the life I want. It feels like I did all this work for nothing.*

Your job is to acknowledge and respect your progress and achievements, no matter how small and no matter how far you still have to go. What you recognize, you get more of. What you ignore goes away.

DOING THE "RIGHT" THINGS ENTITLES YOU TO NOTHING

You read that right.

Following the script, doing exactly as instructed, and taking all the proper steps does not entitle you to success. Unlike what we were taught in school, doing everything "right," or at least what you think is right, is not a free pass to victory. The world, circumstances, and people are always changing, so be prepared to adjust to what's in front of you. Life is fluid, so you must be fluid, too. Make constant adjustments and know things will never stay the same.

Often athletes will tell me how they have "done everything right," but have yet to see the results they had hoped for. Whether the reward you are seeking is a promotion, more playing time on a team, or recognition from team members, there are always elements that people tend to look over. These include:

Being in the right place. Is what you're offering or representing needed where you are right now? The funniest comedian in America probably wouldn't try booking a gig at a funeral home (or hey, maybe that's a great outside-the-box idea).

Arriving at the right time. Why would your product or service be valuable today? What urgent need does it meet? It could be too soon or too late. There were times I was shopping my services as a basketball player for my next professional playing contract when a team would tell me that though they liked my playing abilities, they had already signed a player who played the same position as me. Right place, wrong time.

Having the right skills. You may be very good, even great, at what you do—but do your skills fit the needs of those you are offering them to? Maybe you're getting in front of the wrong people with the right stuff. An athlete can be a very good player, but if he's not very good relative to his teammates, he won't be playing. Maybe he's on the wrong team.

DON'T LET THE 10 PERCENT HOLD YOU BACK

Michael Jordan broke his foot early in his second NBA season. According to his book *Driven from Within*, with only a 10 percent chance of reinjury and a handful of games remaining, Michael received clearance from team doctors to play again.

Michael saw the prognosis as a green light to come back and play those last few games. Playing basketball was his job after all, right? Why *not* play when he's already 90 percent healthy? The Bulls front office didn't see things that way. They didn't want to see Michael injured again and suggested he sit out the remainder of that season. They wanted him back at 100 percent the following season.

Michael didn't want to hear that.

A meeting was held between Michael, his agent, and members of Bulls management. Management reasoned that the 10 percent chance of reinjury was a good enough reason to keep Michael out for the remainder of the season. The Bulls didn't want to put their most valuable asset and best player at risk. Michael had a different mentality. All he wanted to do was get back on the court and help his team as soon as possible. He wasn't worried about the possibility of injury, which, logically, could happen to any player at any time.

After a fruitless back-and-forth, Chicago Bulls general manager Jerry Krause presented an analogy to Michael. Imagine you have a really bad headache and someone handed you a vial of Advil with ten pills in it. But, they explained, one of those ten pills was coated with deadly cyanide.

After presenting this story to Michael, Jerry asked him if he would take one of those pills for his migraine.

Michael thought for a second and replied that while Jerry had posed a hell of an analogy, his answer would depend on how bad the headache was.

Michael Jordan played the rest of that season for the Chicago Bulls, and the team made the playoffs. There, Jordan had his now-legendary 63-point game against the eventual champion Celtics.

An NBA regular season consists of 82 games. Barring his injury-plagued second season and baseball-hiatus shortened 1994–95 season, Michael Jordan played 11 full seasons as a member of the Chicago Bulls. Of 902 possible games, Michael missed 7. Do you think there were days when Michael was bruised and beat up, and could badly use a day off from the grind of his job and the pressure of being who he was? I'm sure there were. But Michael Jordan needed to play his game more than anything else, and he allowed nothing to stop that.

In my life I've met some people who are directionless, unenergized, and uninteresting. These people have no pressing need to be, do, or have anything. I've also met people like Jordan who get labeled psycho, brainwashed, fanatical, delusional, and militaristic in their commitment. Let me ask you a question. Who would you bet your money on: the crazy, determined fanatic or the unmotivated, lazy drifter? I know who I'd trust there—and I bet you do too.

• • •

The saying goes, "It's easier to calm down a lunatic than it is to revive a dead body." The lunatic believes in something strongly enough to be all-in on it. Whether or not you understand it, you have to at least respect this person's commitment to his or her cause. Could you follow people who are unsure of who they are, which way they're going, or what they believe in? Could you admire a person who never fully commits to anything? I know I couldn't.

Drive, ambition, and determination will always make up for what you lack in certainty. Michael Jordan's drive to get back in the game that season supplied the mental edge needed to negate management's fear of the 10 percent chance of reinjury. While you could argue that this didn't make him 100 percent injury-proof, and you're right, his drive *eliminated the chance of failure from being an objection to action*. Anything could fail—if that's reason enough not to try, you'll never do anything.

Many people just don't feel passionately enough about anything to act on the 10 percent chance; some wouldn't even act on a 90 percent chance. Most people need a 100 percent guarantee of success before doing anything. But as nothing in life is guaranteed, that's the exact reason some people never do anything.

Don't be afraid of the 10 percent. Make the 90 percent guarantee by believing in yourself and the discipline it took to get you where you are.

3

SUPER YOU

Now that you've mastered Discipline—WOYG Principle #1—let's take a look at WOYG Principle #2: Confidence. The next three chapters cover critical aspects of confidence: this chapter will help you believe in yourself, Chapter 4 will help you eliminate performance anxiety and self-consciousness, and Chapter 5 will help you overcome fear of success.

• • •

Confidence is a game changer. Of all of humanity's internal, intangible traits, self-esteem is the one that makes the most difference in what you do and what you achieve.

My favorite athlete of all time, former NFL player Deion Sanders, once said this:

When you look good, you feel good.
When you feel good, you play good.
When you play good, they pay good.

While confidence isn't the *only* thing you need to be successful, confidence unlocks all your abilities and frees you to actually do everything you're capable of. Here's a short list of what you'll do with confidence:

- Demand a higher salary—and get it
- Make new friends
- Win battles you never have to fight
- Attract more of what you want
- Gain people's compliance and cooperation
- Receive favors you didn't ask for
- Be admired by those around you

For more than 13 years, I've taught people how to not only build their confidence, but also to prepare themselves to be at peak confidence and fully display their game when the opportunity is there. And now I'm here to teach you.

INCREASE YOUR CAPACITY FOR BELIEF

My freshman year of college at Penn State Abington, I had a teammate named Steve. Abington was a commuter campus and we lived close to each other, so we would ride together to and from games. Steve was a couple of years older than me, and he'd sometimes dispense advice to me. I remember only one thing Steve told me.

We were riding home after a game, and Steve told me that our coach, whom I'd been bumping heads with often, wanted me to be "The Guy" on the team, but as Steve explained, there were some things that I would need to do to earn that title.

At the time, I knew I was a pretty good basketball player, but I wasn't thinking of anything outside of myself. Eighteen-year-old me just wanted to get better, put up impressive statistics, and maybe have a few dunks to impress the fans. I wasn't thinking of an overall team concept at all. If you remember, I'd spent the entire previous year, as a high school senior, sitting the bench as one of the least valuable players on the roster. Steve's revelation was the first time I'd ever considered that I could be the best player on a basketball team.

• • •

Self-confidence is a belief that you can do something. But why, or how, would you believe you could do something if you've never actually done it before?

The first step to upping your belief is increasing your *capacity* for belief. Answer the following questions about your capacity.

How Far Away Can You Be While Maintaining the Faith?

Belief is easy when you can see yourself making progress, have a support system in place, and are close enough to your outcome to see it. The true test of your capacity for belief is when there's nothing indicating that things are going to work out. It's exactly at this point when you must push yourself to maintain a positive vision and keep your ultimate goal.

This skill is developed only through struggle, and belief through struggle requires faith. I like to define *applied faith* as believing in a vision and actually acting on it.

How mentally tough can you be when no one believes in you but you? The wider and deeper your capacity for belief, the more potential you will have.

ARE YOU A FAN OF YOURSELF?

Growing up, there was a really good basketball player in my neighborhood named Phil. When I started going to Finley Playground at age 14 to play basketball, Phil was already well known as one of the best at the park. Phil was a great outside shooter, and his stocky frame, broad shoulders, and facial hair made me think he was about 19 years old. I was wrong. He was my age, just 14.

I couldn't believe it. How could someone my age be *that* damn good? Although we were the same age, Phil was at a whole different level in the game.

By the time I was 16, Phil and I had gotten to know each other. My game had expanded by then, but Phil was still the best in our age group by a wide margin.

One summer day, as we idled on the benches in the shade next to the courts at Finley, Phil and I were talking about our basketball futures. Well, we talked about *his* sure future, and my hoped-for future. In a moment of reflection, Phil asked, "Dre, don't you wish you had game like me? Do you wish you were known like me?"

Phil wasn't being facetious; he genuinely wanted to know my answer. I told Phil that although I would really like to be known for my skills as he was, I didn't want his ability.

Phil thought on this for a moment and asked a follow-up question. "Why not? Something wrong with my game, Dre?" I responded, "No, there's nothing wrong with your game. I just want to have my *own* game."

I'm not sure Phil really understood what I meant by that. I'm also pretty sure that, like me at 16, he didn't yet have the ability to see things from anyone's perspective but his own. He probably thought me a fool to not want to be like him—he was the best player around, after all. But even then, as a 16-year-old player who had barely made a name for myself at my local park, let alone anywhere else, I knew I had to ride with what I had and maximize it. There was no skill-swapping possibility, nor was it something I wanted.

Over time I cultivated some real-life fans, but I was a fan of myself long before there was any logical reason for me or anyone else to be one. *You* need to have that faith in yourself first, before anyone else will have faith in you. Keep reading, and I'll show you how.

ARE YOU A FAN OF ANYONE ELSE MORE THAN OF YOURSELF?

I use social media regularly and see the debates and conversations people have about professional sports. What has always fascinated me is how passionate some people get when arguing for (or against) their favorite (or least favorite) athletes and teams. People yell, curse, attack random strangers on a personal level, and get more worked up debating the NBA Finals than they ever get about their own lives.

Many people are bigger fans of their idols and favorite players than they are of themselves. These people experience a stronger feeling of winning or losing when their team or player wins than they do when *they* win or lose in their own games.

I'm not saying there's anything wrong with being a fan and rooting for players you like, but when the game is over, it's your turn to create your own fans, starting with yourself. Don't be so much of a fan that you forget to be a player.

What Do You See in Someone Else That You Don't See in You?

I had a teammate my sophomore year of college named Andy. While Penn State Altoona (where I'd been recruited after my freshman year at Abington) was an NCAA D3 school, the basketball team at Penn State's main campus, which was 45 minutes away, was D1. During downtime one day at practice, the topic turned to the D1 team at State College. Andy, who was an average-at-best player on our D3 team, told me that I could never beat any players from the D1 squad.

While Andy was entitled to his (inaccurate) opinion, I couldn't wrap my mind around how someone who plays basketball could think this way. It went against everything I'd known as a competitor. You couldn't see yourself beating someone just because they're on a "higher" team than you? Someone being on a higher-level team was the exact reason why I wanted to face and beat him!

If you're more a fan of someone else than you are of you, there's a gap between what you see in them and what you see in you. Let's address and fill that gap.

Seeing the traits you admire most in other people, ask yourself what they may have done or how they think to acquire those traits. Maybe they were born that way. Ask yourself, *What can I do to acquire these same traits for myself?* Start doing it.

Who Do You Expect the Most from: Yourself or Someone Else?

I've watched basketball games on TV and grown frustrated with an athlete who has underperformed in a big game. I expected more from him and he didn't deliver. Then I catch myself and realize—the same standards I'm holding that guy to, I need to check myself and make sure I expect the same from me. It makes no sense to criticize a person who's failed to live up to standards that I might not even have for myself.

———————————— EXAMINE YOUR GAME ————————————

How high do you set the bar for others, compared to how high you set the bar for yourself?

When Did You Last Defend Yourself the Way You Defend Your Favorite Player, Musician, or Movie Star?

I understand defending someone you admire against unjust criticism, but it's just as important to ask yourself when you last defended yourself with the same passion. If there's any person from whom you expect more than you expect of yourself, you can never fulfill your potential. If you defend or get excited about anyone else more than you'll defend or get excited for yourself, you'll have a hard time creating and keeping fans.

If you're not a fan of yourself, don't expect anyone else to be the first.

YOU CAN'T "FAKE IT"— YOU CAN ONLY MAKE IT

But what if you haven't actually *done* anything yet that gives you a reason to believe in yourself? How do you get started with all this confidence stuff? Maybe you've heard of "Fake It 'Til You Make It" (FITYMI). The premise of FITYMI is pretending that you're something or someone else until you actually become that.

The very idea of FITYMI spawns many questions:

- *Does it really work?*
- *How do I do it?*
- *Could it actually hurt me in the long run?*
- *Why would anyone ever want to be fake?*

Before you think of the answers, let me tell you something: FITYMI is a myth. There's no such thing as *faking it until you make it*.

Here's why: As soon as you decide to be someone other than who you are, you're no longer faking. It becomes 100 percent real.

• • •

A high school basketball coach tried an experiment one day at practice. He explained: "Today, each of you players is going to pretend to be one of your teammates. This way you can show your teammate how he plays—the good, the bad, and the ugly."

One particular player, let's call him Tim, was maybe the ninth or tenth best player on the 12-man roster. Tim was randomly assigned to portray his teammate Mike. Mike just happened to be the best player on the team, their leading scorer, and a future D1 college player.

What happened next?

Tim played better that day than he had ever played. His teammates were shocked, and Tim even surprised himself. At the end of practice, Tim's coach said, "If that's what it takes to make you play the way you just did, you need to pretend to be Mike *every* day."

• • •

Human beings can focus on only one thing at a time. If you use FITYMI from now on exactly as I explain it to you, you can't possibly be faking. You'll actually be *being* and *doing* it—no fakery involved.

The change—from who you have been to who you need or want to be—is not a gradual process; it happens the instant you decide to enact change and lasts for as long as you're willing to keep it up.

To *have* anything you want in life, you must pay the price by *doing* what needs to be done, right? For example:

- To have money, you work, sell, barter, etc.
- To have great health, you eat smart and exercise regularly.
- To have friends, you invest in relationships.

Everyone understands and agrees on this equation of *doing something in order to have something* (though not everyone practices it). Ask 10 random people if they agree, and they would likely concur.

But . . . wait a minute.

There are a lot of hardworking people out there, though, who adhere to this equation faithfully—yet they *don't* have what they want. Do they need something else? What's missing? Knowledge? Strategy? Help?

"Be-Do-Have"

There's a life achievement principle known as "Be-Do-Have" that says that who you are *being* determines and colors everything you *do*, which leads to your *results* (or the lack thereof).

A lot of good, honest people work hard for their entire lives. However, many of these people jump into the work—the

Doing—without asking themselves who they need to *Be* to achieve their goals. Since they never ask, they never *become* this person and, despite everything they *DO*, they never *HAVE* what they want, even though they *DID* all the right things.

Reread the above paragraph, and ask yourself these questions:

- Does this describe anyone you know?
- Do you know any good, hardworking people who never seem to get ahead or ever have anything they want?
- Have you ever heard of (or been) a person complaining that they "did everything right," yet still didn't get what they wanted, and can't figure out why?

FITYMI is not real. The desired results of what we call FITYMI are principles of *being*, not faking. What does that mean? You can't *fake* doing things. If I point to a chair and tell you to sit in it, there's no faking it: you either sit in the chair or you don't. When Tim shot the ball that fateful day in practice and it went in the basket, those weren't fake points—they were real. When executed properly (and I'll show you how), *being* alters who you are as a person, which affects your actions, which lead to a result.

Therefore, there is no such thing as *Fake* It 'Til You Make It. You simply make it.

EXAMINE YOUR GAME

As soon as you give yourself permission to *become* something or someone, you've made it. It's 1,000 percent real. There is no fakery involved.

Why Some People Think FITYMI Doesn't Work

Let me illustrate an example of how people take this FITYMI concept out of context, use it incorrectly, don't get their desired result, then blame the method for their failure (*FITYMI doesn't work!*).

Suppose you have a friend—we'll call him Mark—who wants to work on his confidence. Here's a step-by-step process that Mark uses to become more confident:

1. Mark has battled confidence issues all his life, yet he still wants to be more confident. And he's serious about it this time.

2. Learning about FITYMI, Mark decides to put it to work and *fake* his confidence for a few days, or even stretch it to a few weeks, if things go well. Mark will employ the strategy starting at work, where he's a car salesman.

3. Mark fakes his confidence while talking with his supervisors and coworkers. The thing is, Mark's coworkers know Mark well, so they easily see through his weak facade. They make fun of Mark, and they urge him to quit the act: *What are you doing, reading self-help books on your days off, Mark? You're good enough as you are, man! Being fake isn't cool. Be yourself, Mark!*

4. Undeterred by the haters, Mark tries using his new faked confidence dealing with people who don't know him from anywhere else: new customers who walk into the dealership showroom. The problem is, Mark is now of two minds: one where he has to *fake* his confidence with customers, while the other defaults to the "normal" (un-self-confident) Mark when he deals with people he knows already. This inefficient attempt at multitasking

(which, by definition, is inefficient) means Mark is not good at either one: his fake-confident self *or* his normal, nonconfident self.

5. No one believes Mark's FITYMI act. It doesn't help him at work. Being this contrived version of himself, Mark actually sells *fewer* cars than he did before. Mark has the poor results to prove that FITYMI doesn't work.

6. Mark swears off FITYMI and hypnotizes himself (because every thought, word, and feeling you have is self-hypnosis) into believing that the normal, pre-FITYMI Mark—the one he swore on improving—is now good enough, since he obviously can't change himself.

7. Mark lives out the remainder of an underwhelming life with a diminished, uncompelling level of self-belief, which seeps into everything he does.

8. Mark takes his talent and potential to the most valuable real estate on the planet: the graveyard.

Does that sound like fun?

What Mark Did Wrong in Trying to "Fake" Confidence and Success

Mark made several mistakes. Before you read my explanation of what these mistakes were, along with a revised plan for Mark to do things correctly, go back and see how many errors you can point out. I explain Mark's errors below.

Mistake #1: Mark put an end date on his FITYMI experiment. Here's a Mental Toughness word you'll learn in Chapter 6: *Until.* If you've DECIDED to be, do, or have something, that means you're committed to making it happen, and you'll persist UNTIL it works—not IF it works—and you'll change your approach when necessary.

And remember: concepts, programs, and ideas don't work. The only thing that works is YOU.

Mistake #2: Mark decided to use FITYMI . . . _if_ things went well. Mark was not _committed_ to making his experiment go well; no wonder it didn't. When you're truly committed to an outcome, there's nothing you won't do to make that outcome a reality.

In my pursuit of a basketball career, I made many decisions that were illogical, financially foolish, and straight-up reckless. I spent the last money I had on gas, a shared hotel room, and camp fee to go to the first exposure camp where my basketball career began. I could have saved the money and maybe moved out of my parents' home instead. I sold gym memberships at Bally and passed on more stable, higher-paying jobs because I knew I'd need maximum flexibility if and when a basketball opportunity presented itself. I knew these choices seemed unwise when I was doing them and didn't care, because I was committed to the outcome and to making my next playing opportunity happen.

When you step into anything with an "if it works" mentality, you're giving yourself an "out clause"—yet the presence of the "out clause" is the exact reason it won't work.

In contrast, think of times in your life when pressure was on and you _had_ to make something happen. You were, by default, fully committed. Without my even knowing what that situation was in your life, I know that you made it happen. How do I know? Commitment brings a magic power with it that moves obstacles out of our way. Mark's lack of commitment from the very beginning was the exact reason he fell short.

Mistake #3: Mark tried using FITYMI at work, but nowhere else in his life. This is confidence multitasking, which we know doesn't work. Have you heard the saying "how you do anything is how you do everything"? Mark wanted to limit his confidence experiment to certain parts of life (probably where Mark felt it would be safe to do so), leaving his one-track mind (which we all have) confused as to what the true program was. *Are we confident or not?*

Mark was on the confidence version of a diet. All diets have one inherent problem: they *end*. And when they end, people go back to their former habits.

Mistake #4: Mark's FITYMI plan was based on everything working in his favor. Mark did not consider how much negativity and ridicule he'd be subject to for trying to be someone other than who he had been to that point, or for trying to better himself. Mark hadn't planned how he would resist that negativity and ridicule.

Mistake #5: Mark never truly believed in his FITYMI experiment. He would have been better off doing nothing from the beginning and using his time some other way. If you're not fully CONVINCED of your ability to win, *trying* is a waste of time.

As my first basketball coach said at our first team gathering, *there are no tryouts, just the first day of practice.* Mark's efforts landed him in the same place he'd started.

Mistake #6: Mark quit and decided not to try again. That makes Mark a loser. Even though Mark's strategies sucked, and he should have read this book before he began his confidence-building work, his decision to not try again—because his strategy "didn't work"—starts Mark on a lifelong path of failure and defeat.

Success means to be in the pursuit of goals. Failure exists only in having no goals, thus nothing to pursue. Mark wanted more confidence, but he decided to stop going when FITYMI "didn't work."

Not going after something that you know you want makes you a loser.

How to *Really* Become Self-Confident

So let's redo Mark's FITYMI experiment, the right way this time.

1. Mark has battled confidence issues all his life. But now he's serious about overcoming this challenge, once and for all.

2. Understanding what I explain in his chapter, Mark gets clear not only on what outcome he wants and what he will do to get it, but also who he needs to be as a person to do these things. Mark asks the *Who do I need to be?* question of himself over and over again, until he gets the answers that correspond to the actions that will produce his desired result.

3. Mark writes down his answers to the *Who do I need to BE?* question. Mark reads the answers aloud to himself daily. This repetition leads to the creation of habits of being that create unconscious changes in Mark as a person. People around Mark notice subtle differences in Mark that are hard to point out, but they can feel a change in his energy.

WORK ON YOUR GAME

4. In meeting new people as his new self, Mark grows even more in his confidence. The new people Mark meets don't know anything about his past self-esteem issues, so they can only address and regard Mark as Mark has been presented to them: the poised and confident man in front of them. As more and more people see and treat Mark this way, Mark's confidence grows even more.

5. People who have known Mark for years begin making remarks about his increased confidence and improved posture. Mark (who has conditioned himself to be this new version of himself) is happy to admit that he has changed as a person. Because Mark is not faking his being, having others notice and comment about it emboldens Mark to take it further and see how it can work in other areas of his life.

6. Mark applies this FITYMI principle to his eating habits, his personal relationships, his finances, and his work life.

7. Mark becomes the person he wants to be, making a note to thank Dre when he wins the Nobel Prize for Greatness.

Who you're being as a person cannot be faked. As multitasking requires small bursts of attention, who you're *being* is who you *are*, at least for the moment. That means you can change who you're being at any moment, and you can make it permanent with the proper conditioning.

Now that you understand leveraging FITYMI, how can you max out on confidence as quickly and efficiently as possible?

MAXIMIZE YOUR CONFIDENCE

If your confidence were 25 times higher, what would you be doing differently? Ask yourself these questions—and write down the answers below:

- *Who would I talk to?*

  _____

  _____

- *What chances would I take?*

  _____

  _____

- *What responsibilities would I take on?*

  _____

  _____

- *What would I stop doing?*

  _____

  _____

- *What relationships would I end?*

  _____

  _____

- *What would I no longer tolerate?*

  _____

  _____

- *What inconveniences would I eliminate?*

  _____

  _____

- *Where would I stop procrastinating?*

  _____

  _____

The world is full of highly skilled people, but it's likely you'll never hear of most of them because of their lack of confidence to put their skill fully out there in the world. Let's look at some situations in which believing in yourself is necessary:

- To walk away from a comfortable yet unfulfilling long-term relationship, you need the confidence to believe you can stand on your own, support yourself in every way, and find love elsewhere.
- To quit a sport you've been playing forever, you need sufficient self-esteem to deal with the reactive comments of people who think they know what's best for you, and to deal with your own self-judgment over quitting something that you know isn't right for you.
- If you're terminally unhappy at your job, but don't have another situation lined up, it takes guts to quit with no fallback plan (not that this is the best option for everyone).

When you see people unwilling to stop doing something that *they* know is hurting them, their concern is that the alternative won't live up to their expectations.

WRITE YOUR SCRIPT

At your highest confidence level, ask yourself these questions:

- *How do I look?*
- *Where do I live?*
- *Who are my friends?*
- *What do people say about me?*
- *What do I do every day?*
- *What kind of family do I have?*
- *What does my house and car look like?*

With these questions in mind, describe yourself at your best:

_____

_____

_____

_____

_____

_____

_____

_____

_____

You probably answered all these questions in a very positive way. Even better, you *control* all these things. So, upping your confidence is easy (read: *doable*). Start being this person now—and stay there.

Award-winning actors become someone else for a living, and they get paid well to do so. By reading this section, you've stepped on set. The studio has wired an advance to you for your work. If you don't fulfill your role, they'll demand their money back. So start doing your damn job!

Now, actors don't do it all alone. Other actors play supporting roles. Sets are constructed specifically for filming. Maybe some city streets get blocked off, or a public park is closed for shooting. Even with no one role-playing with you, you need to build your set.

Write a list of your best accomplishments, the parts of your life that you're most proud of:

_____

_____

_____

_____

_____

_____

_____

_____

_____

_____

_____

_____

_____

Next, create a separate list of all the reasons you *deserve* to raise your confidence:

_____

_____

_____

_____

_____

_____

_____

_____

_____

_____

_____

_____

_____

_____

_____

_____

_____

_____

_____

_____

_____

Grab photographs, trophies, and awards that remind you of your proudest moments. Look at them often to remind you of your greatness.

If your life is to become a great movie—a movie that inspires others to become more themselves and is watched again and again long after you're gone—you need to give your best performance in playing the leading role. Build a set that makes everything believable and real to you and to everyone else.

Follow the above steps, and people who have never heard of you will rush to the theaters to see what all the fuss is about.

• • •

What about when you *feel* fully confident, but the lights come on and you freeze up? What if pregame jitters and performance anxiety have hurt your game when it matters most?

We have a fix for that: I cover it in the next chapter.

4

———•———————————•———

ELIMINATE SELF-CONSCIOUSNESS AND PERFORMANCE ANXIETY, FOREVER

Building confidence requires not only believing in yourself but also getting rid of self-consciousness and anxiety. Easier said than done, I know.

▬▬▬KNOW HOW YOUR MIND WORKS:▬▬▬ CONSCIOUSLY, UNCONSCIOUSLY, AND SELF-CONSCIOUSLY

To better understand *self-consciousness*, let's first consider the different functions of the conscious mind and the unconscious mind. When I became interested in this topic (and neuroscience in general), I learned that 95 percent of our brain activity—such as breathing, digestion, and blinking—is beyond conscious awareness.* Therefore, a lot of our survival as humans is owed to unconscious brain and body functioning. In fact, if we were able to choose between conscious or unconscious control for our most vital functions, we'd be wise to keep it the way it is— unconscious—for no other reason than to keep that work off our brains.

Humans' super-developed brains and conscious thoughts gave us power over plants and animals. Conscious thinking is responsible for the device or paper you're reading this on, the vehicles you ride in, the clothing you wear. But despite the creative, forward-thinking power of our conscious mind, it's also fully responsible in every instance where we mess things up— *every single time.*

In contrast, have you ever forgotten to breathe?

Have you ever deliberately disrupted the timing of your heartbeat?

Has procrastination ever kept you from digesting your food?

Whomever or whatever created us wisely didn't leave our conscious minds in control of the critical functions that matter most to our survival.

Which brings us to self-consciousness, the state of being *too conscious*—in other words, thinking too much. When our conscious minds volunteer to take on work that they were never asked to do in the first place, the unconscious cannot do what it does best.

• • •

---

* Marc Van Rymenant, "95% of Brain Activity Is Beyond Our Conscious Awareness," simplifyinginterfaces.com, August 1, 2008, http://www.simplifyinginterfaces.com/2008/08 /01/95-percent-of-brain-activity-is-beyond-our-conscious-awareness/.

I played basketball with a lot of talented players. Some of them (despite of or maybe because of their talent) were not very fun to play with. One of these players was a guy I'll call Gus.

Every time I saw him play, Gus was the most talented player on the court. The problem was, Gus played the game as if there was no one else on his team, angling for his own personal shine and passing the ball only when there was no other option. It was hard to play with Gus because everyone was a mere accessory to his personal show. Sometimes, especially in team sports, a player's personal ambitions take a backseat to the success of the team. But Gus couldn't enjoy the team winning if he was not the focal point of the action; in fact, I would suspect that Gus would rather have a great individual game and lose rather than have an OK game and win. Gus was a damn good player, but he was all about himself.

When it comes to life, Gus is the conscious mind and the other four players are the unconscious. *Self-consciousness* is Gus, the one "conscious" player who tries to do everything himself, which results in him shunning his teammates and never passing the ball. His four teammates are the unconscious mind. They are left to stand idly and watch, unable to make much impact on the game. The ball-hogging conscious mind takes everything in his own hands, tries to do too much, and can cost the team the game in the process.

●────────────── EXAMINE YOUR GAME ──────────────●

Get rid of *self-consciousness* by letting your
unconscious mind do what it does best.

●──●

HANDLING PERFORMANCE ANXIETY

This is self-consciousness: trying to score on five defenders when you have four wide-open teammates. *Self-consciousness* before or during a game, speech, date, or sales presentation, somewhere you know you're being watched and evaluated, is better known as *performance anxiety*.

When I was 17 and playing in a recreational league, my team made it all the way to the championship game. I had been playing the best basketball of my life to that point, and a well-known coach at Simon Gratz High School named Bill Ellerbee had been sitting on the sideline near our bench during the semifinal game.

"That was some nice shooting," he said after the game, and I thanked him. I learned from one of my teammates that Coach Ellerbee was at the game on a scouting mission—and after my solid semifinal performance, I was on his radar. To go from not making my high school team at E&S to getting recruited to Gratz, the top Public League team in Philadelphia at the time, would have been a hell of a story. It was possible that I was just one game away from it being a reality.

In the championship game of the league, we played against Cherashore Playground, a team we hadn't faced in the regular season. They had watched our semifinal win and knew what they needed to do: not let me shoot any threes and stop our other top scorer, whom Coach Ellerbee was scouting as well.

The first play of the championship game, I caught the ball in the corner. Cherashore's defender ran out to me hard, hard enough that I dribbled (something I'd rarely done that season) twice to my right along the baseline and made a 10-foot pull-up jumper to start the game. I had not executed a move like that all year. I'd surprised everyone in the gym—including myself—with this opening shot and basket.

Too bad the buckets ended there.

I finished the game with just that 2 points, and we suffered our only loss of the season in the league championship game. I shot the same shots I had been shooting all year, but they just weren't going in. With every miss, I created more pressure to make the next one. I could feel everyone watching me, and I imagined that they were wondering what the problem was.

I had choked.

I hadn't felt any nervousness before the game. If anything, I was excited. I knew many people were going to be watching me, and I fully expected to dominate in front of the large crowd. Up to that point in the season, I had come through for my team every time, but all that really matters is the end result—and I had not delivered.

I didn't *feel* anxious, but maybe I was. Maybe I had put too much pressure on myself, knowing what was at stake. Maybe I had made myself anxious, thinking too much about what I stood to gain and all I wanted to prove.

You have been in situations like this. You practiced, studied, and prepared for this moment. You knew what to expect from yourself. Then the game came, and you were a deer caught in the headlights. You had sweaty palms, your nerves were out of control, and you felt super-self-conscious about your every word and movement. You felt like everyone was watching, judging you, and thinking the worst of you. These thoughts showed in your performance.

You don't understand how you could have practiced so much and had so much skill, then got to showtime and seemingly lost it all.

Is there something you can do about it?

Think of your game and the skills you've developed as a tool-box. We're all born with an empty toolbox, so you must *Work*

On Your Game by practicing, training, learning, and investing in yourself to fill your box with as many tools as possible. The more you practice, the more tools you own.

Unfortunately, this is about as far as many people get. Then they're baffled when their skills don't show when they're most needed.

There are two reasons why this happens.

Reason #1: Having WOYG Tools Is Not Enough: You Need to *Use* Them!

The tools you've amassed are no different from your memories of the past, or information you've learned in school or from books. Your mind has an unlimited storage capacity for more and more of both. But that doesn't mean you're always *thinking* of everything you know or everything you've seen.

Think about what you were doing this month, five years ago. Consider where you were geographically, who you were spending time with, and what you spent most of your time doing.

Now think of your first week at the last job you held before your current one, or your first friend at the last school you attended. Notice how you probably had not considered these memories in quite some time, yet how quickly they came to you when you asked for them. Also note how, if I had not brought them to your attention, you probably wouldn't have thought of them today.

In other words, you have skills that are ready when called on, but *only if you call on them*. Just because you've practiced a skill does not mean that skill will show up when you need it.

One of the YouTube videos I created to help people improve their basketball skills was a 60-second video called "Simple Daily Dribbling Drills." It was a basketball dribbling practice series that any player could do each day to become a solid ball handler. At the end of the quick demonstration, I left viewers with a simple message: "Do these drills every day for five years and you'll have Handle." ("Handle" meaning solid basketball dribbling ability.)

The #1 comment I always got on that video was this:

Damn, Dre, FIVE YEARS??? Do I REALLY have to practice for that long to be good?

Some players who hadn't seen the video would ask me straight up: "How long did you have to work on your handle to be good at dribbling?"

I tell you the same thing I told them:

You must continue to work on your skills for as long as you wish to have them at your disposal.

Reason #2: Know *How* to Use Your Tools the Right Way, at the Right Time

While Working On Your Game is a requirement for success, you must know how to *use* your game. Having a lot of skill is not the end of your work—it's the beginning of your work.

Think of that imaginary toolbox again. Let's say you splurged at Home Depot and bought every single tool imaginable, ensuring you could fix anything in your home, by yourself, without calling for help. You have every tool a home could ever need.

Does this mean you can fix anything that breaks?

Hell, no!

Performing at your best is not a matter of mere skill *accumulation*. You need to know *how*, *when*, and *where* to use what you've accumulated, and when *not* to use it.

And all of this needs to be unconsciously controlled, keeping your conscious mind safely out of the way. Make that happen, and self-consciousness and performance anxiety are permanently banned.

To do this, adopt the following principles to condition your unconscious mind.

BE BOLD! SELF-CONSCIOUSNESS IS INNER-DIRECTED; BOLDNESS IS OUTER-DIRECTED

When you're self-conscious, you're constantly conscious of what you're doing, thinking about how you're doing it, and worrying what others are thinking and saying about you (usually nothing, as they're not even focused on you in the slightest). Self-consciousness repels people, luck, and good fortune because you're keeping all your energy and focus for yourself. It's directed inward, only to you.

Because most of our functions—such as walking, biking, sitting, standing, and even casually talking—are best done unconsciously, self-consciousness makes every little thing we do feel incredibly awkward. I'm sure you've noticed this in other people. Self-consciousness is a self-fulfilling mindset: the more self-conscious people notice others noticing them, the more they think they are being judged. Thus, the more self-conscious they become, which leads to more awkward behaviors, and the more people actually do notice them and their awkwardness.

Self-consciousness is a selfish energy: all we can think about is ourselves. When we are self-conscious, we cannot attract positive energy because we're hoarding all our resources for ourselves.

Conversely, boldness is a confident energy that provides so much internal assurance that you can afford to direct focus outward instead of at yourself. Boldness causes you to radiate energy that people can feel. And because you're sending out so much energy, you receive energy back from people and environments. It's the law of karma in effect.

I once saw Jay-Z perform in Miami. After opening with a song, he addressed the audience. The first thing he said was, "I want to share something with you tonight." He went on to sprinkle a few inspirational messages in between a two-hour medley of his hit songs. Jay-Z wasn't concerned with what anyone thought of his wardrobe or if someone didn't like his set list that night. He was performing not in the mindset of *I hope they like me*, but in the spirit of giving—giving his energy, music, presence, and appreciation for the audience. He wasn't there to *take* by being preoccupied with what everyone was thinking about him. I watched the audience throughout the show and saw how much energy all the fans had in singing and dancing along to his music. The crowd more than gave back, because Jay-Z was giving so much of himself.

Similarly, pop star Beyoncé had an onstage alter ego named Sasha Fierce whom she became before a live performance. "I turn into Sasha. I wouldn't like Sasha if I met her off stage. She's too aggressive, too strong, too sassy, too sexy! I'm not like her in real life at all. I'm not flirtatious and super-confident and fearless like her. What I feel onstage I don't feel anywhere else. It's an out-of-body experience. I created my stage persona . . . so that when I go home, I don't have to think about what it is I do. Sasha isn't me. The people around me know who I really am."*

---

* Jody Thompson, "Beyoncé Explains Her Alter-Ego Sasha Fierce . . . ," The Mirror online, November 27, 2008, https://www.mirror.co.uk/3am/celebrity-news/beyonce-explains-her-alter-ego-sasha-fierce-362578.

When I give a speech at events, I don't worry about the toolbox. I know my material well—including my stories, key points, and takeaways; I even anticipate when the audience will laugh (though I'm not always right). When I get onstage I know I'm being watched, and because I know my game and know its value, that attention doesn't make me self-conscious—it excites me! Like Jay-Z said, I get to *share* what I have with my audience, and they give energy back to me.

The same is true in business. A truly great salesperson is purely focused on what he or she can give, not on what the salesperson stands to get.

Think about your own life and experience:

- Haven't you done your best when you were bold and outer-directed with your energy?
- Didn't you give your best performance and have your best games when you were calmly radiating energy outward to the point that you completely forgot about yourself?
- Think of a time when your performance looked and felt effortless.

Have you ever caught yourself consciously thinking about something that you usually do without thinking, and clumsily fumbled a bit in doing it? It could be something as mundane as tying your shoes or writing your name. That's what happens when our (relatively) slow, clunky conscious minds get too focused on the self and interrupt the smooth, instantaneous work of our subconscious minds.

Excitement and self-consciousness are the exact same
energy, with a small difference: Excitement is directed
outward; self-consciousness is directed *inward*.
If you hoard your energy and only direct it inward,
it will grow stale from lack of circulation.
Instead, send energy outward and you will get it back.

ENJOY THE ATTENTION: WHEN PEOPLE ARE WATCHING YOU, TALKING ABOUT YOU, AND JUDGING YOU, THEY SHOULD BE!

Most people are boring.

They do boring things, work at boring jobs (or, more accurately stated, they *make* their jobs boring), think boring thoughts, and lead generally uninteresting lives. They're never very excited about anything, and nothing exciting or noteworthy ever comes from them. I hope some of those people read this book and help themselves.

When you're being watched, you are the show.

As humans, we have a need for stimulation; even boring people need it. To an audience, you represent energy, excitement, and something worthy of attention (it doesn't need to be positive attention). Boring people will certainly watch, discuss, admire, hate, and otherwise judge you.

And they should.

You're a bold individual whose energy changes a room the second you walk into it. Your presence alone requires attention. Be thankful for boring people: they are the audience that makes the stage what it is. You serve a very important purpose for people who live in the audience. Be happy and thankful for them. They need something to pay attention to and talk about; they damn sure couldn't talk about themselves. Appreciate and indulge them.

With all that attention, you are bound to piss someone off for some irrational reason. The more attention is on you, the higher the chance someone disapproves. Therefore, it is important to know the next principle.

STOP SEEKING APPROVAL

To reach success and achieve our goals, we need far fewer outside approvals than we think we do. Some people try way too hard to gain approval from others. The problem with that is, even when you're successful at winning people's approval, you lose. A person can respect you only so much when you've bent over backward for his or her admiration. And as bending over backwards can be physically uncomfortable, you'll eventually straighten up and be who you truly are, running the risk of those won-over people no longer approving of you.

Well, this is a lot of information to process. How do you remember all this stuff before you hit the stage, court, or boardroom?

You don't.

When It's Time to Perform, Thinking Is Not on the Menu

You're already ready.

You earned your spot.

You're here for a reason.

People are supposed to be watching you—that's the reason you work on your game.

When it's showtime, focus on your audience and how you'll give them your best, and they'll respond in kind. If you keep it all for yourself, you'll get nothing back.

Here's your Preperformance Checklist:

Remind yourself how you got here. You're performing in a big moment for a reason. You've proven yourself enough that now, with something on the line, you've been called on to deliver. Everything you've been through to this point, even the stuff you didn't want, was part of the setup. You're not here by accident. Mentally embrace the fact that you earned your spot; there is no one better suited to be here than you are. Get ready to perform as someone who belongs where you are.

Find your Mental Zone: get there and stay there. The Mental Zone is a state of mind where everything slows down around you and your actions are effortless. You're controlling life like you would play a video game:

- For a speaker or presenter, this zone is the perfect combination of words coming to you at just the right moment.
- For an athlete, it's when every move and shot just happens on its own; you cannot miss.
- For an entertainer, your every idea becomes a hit addition to your performance; there's no struggle or grind to the work.
- For a workplace professional, this is when no task drags on, there's no late-afternoon crash, and you breeze through workdays.

We each have our own zone triggers: certain ideas, thoughts, people, sounds, images, and other stimuli that help move us to the state of flow where everything is easy. Think of your own experiences being in that zone and deconstruct them:

- What got you there mentally?
- How can you recreate that scenario in your mind?
- How can you practice getting there so you can do it on-call?

Take 10 deep breaths, while envisioning your successful performance. Deep breathing can lower stress and anxiety, facilitate calmness, and improve blood circulation and focus. Deep breaths go down into your abdomen and expand your belly, not your chest. Allow all the oxygen to expand your stomach. Breathe in for eight seconds, hold your breath for four seconds, then breathe out for eight seconds.

Can you feel your body beginning to relax? Take 10 of these deep breaths before your performance and feel the calm, focused energy that comes with it.

Go out and show your game. Execute what you've been practicing. That's it.

"I GOT THIS": HOW YOUR CONFIDENCE AFFECTS AND INFLUENCES OTHERS

There's a crucial situation at hand. You can feel the pressure and tension mounting. Everyone is wondering who's going to step up and lead.

You're the person to do it. You step up and take charge, tell everyone what you need them to do, and they gladly follow your lead. One reason is your certainty. The other is that no one else wants all that pressure on him or her.

"I got this."

I'll show you how to use this mindset to calm and ready your team and yourself.

Understand that this mindset can be used only by people who are 100 percent sure they know what they're doing, where they're going, and how they will get it done.

Belief in yourself is the first step. This mindset starts not with how you see a situation, but with how you see yourself:

- Are you a powerful person?
- Are you capable of making anything happen, handling any situation, able to find the light in the darkest of darkness?
- Is there anything that can defeat you and cause you to quit?
- Are you willing and able to persist longer and more strongly than anyone else around you?

Here's what happens when you enact "I Got This."

You Take the Pressure off of Everyone Else

When the team is facing a tough situation, the pressure of figuring out—and executing on—how to handle it is the last thing most people want on their shoulders. When you step up to take responsibility, no one is going to fight you for it. They happily get behind you and let you lead the way. If things go bad, the blame will be on you.

If you want leadership, take it when times are toughest.

Everyone Else Can Focus on What Each Does Best

When you take responsibility and own that leadership post, you not only relieve everyone else from having to do it, you also free those people to do what they do best and nothing more. Asking people to give more than they may be capable of is an inexact science. While some may step up to the challenge, some will fold, and others may believe they're doing all they can and are being pushed too hard, too fast. Your job is assuring them that they need to do only what they've been doing, while you handle the rest and take up the slack.

This is how leadership works: you set the example by doing more than you have to, and others will be infected by your energy and do the same. Your presence allows everyone else to focus on their job, never pressed to stretch past their limitations. As long as they do their job, they know you will handle the rest.

And who wants to slack off when the top person is out there giving his or her all?

You Give Yourself a Call to Action to Figure It Out and Make It Happen

Does your stepping up mean everything will just work itself out? No. You still have to do the work. You said you got it; now "get" it. For you, putting yourself in the "I got this" frame of mind is a call to action to find and execute a solution.

Wait, isn't that really risky? Saying you're going to handle something, without any real idea of how you're going to do it?

Well, yeah. Which is why leaders are so rare.

— EXAMINE YOUR GAME —

Instead of listening to all the noise, learn to listen to yourself.

THROUGH THE BONES

We all like to sing—at home, that is. Or in the shower, in the car, or when no one's close by. There is a saying that TV cameras add 15 pounds to anyone's physique; if you've ever listened to your own voice on audio or video, you may have noticed the audio version of those 15 pounds. According to bioengineer Dr. Tobias Reichenbach, the sound of our own voice, traveling through our *bones* from the mouth to the brain, sounds completely different when traveling through headphones or speakers and traveling through *air*.*

Sounds we hear from the outside (meaning any device or person who is not us) travel through air. When we speak and hear ourselves, *that* sound travels through bones. To overcome performance anxiety and build your confidence, you need to understand the difference.

When I was a teen, my influences were my parents, teachers, a handful of family members, and maybe some well-respected, influential neighbors. Today, you may have some of the same influences, but there are also many more. There is so much material and so many opinions traveling through the air, sifting through it all and deciding whom to give a shot or pay attention to, much less whom to really listen to and follow, is a job all in itself. The space for anyone to share their point of view is widening and deepening.

Which is why, starting now and even more urgently tomorrow and the next day, you must know how and when to listen to sound coming through the bones versus sound traveling through air.

---

* Colin Smith, "Scientists Explain in More Detail How We Hear via Bones in the Skull," imperial.ac.uk, July 9, 2014, https://www.imperial.ac.uk/news/153374/scientists-explain -more-detail-hear-bones.

The air is everything coming from other people: opinions, examples, advice. Is there any value in this stuff? Hopefully so, as this very book, to you, is through-the-air material. You can learn a lot and save yourself time and effort if you're wise in choosing what to listen to through the air.

But "the air" also carries pollution. The very things holding you back in life—fear, bad habits, bad examples modeled by losers—come to you through the air. You weren't born hesitant or self-conscious. You learned it.

Your bones, on the other hand, naturally speak truth. Your instincts, the destiny that awaits you, those "gut feelings" that you just can't shake—all travel "through the bones." The problem for many of us is that we've taken in so much "through the air" that it dangerously contaminates anything traveling through our bones. Consider this:

- Have you ever had a crazy idea that no one other than you believed in?
- Have you ever seen something in your mind that you couldn't accurately describe to anyone, thus you couldn't get anyone on-board with your vision?
- Have you ever gone so far out on a limb for something you believed in that other people urged you not to do so, out of concern for your safety and security?

When people aren't hearing or understanding you, even if you're being completely rational and logical, remember: your words are reaching them *through the air*. What you hear *through the bones* applies only to you. You need to reconnect with the most important sounds, those traveling through your bones.

Let's identify the "sounds" you'll be dealing with.

Opinions

Opinions seem to be the only thing that everyone believes they're entitled to give. Everyone is entitled to confidence, getting better, setting goals, being happy, and expanding their comfort zones, yet opinions are the only thing 100 percent of us indulge in. Why? Unlike getting better, opinions are easy—they require little effort and carry no accountability. They're easy to acquire and widely available. For the same reasons, opinions are the least valuable resource in the air, and they should be held up to strictest scrutiny before being allowed into your system.

"Shoulds"

These are the things others say you *should* do; they indicate obligation, duty, or correctness. "Shoulds" always travel through the air, never through the bones. Even the ones we think we've made up ourselves are picked up from goals other people set for us (*You're how old and not married yet? When are you having kids? You're that tall and can't dunk?*), comparing our progress with someone else's (*I need to [do X] like [so-and-so] does*), and chasing objectives that we don't even want to reach but we think will garner admiration and acceptance. "Shoulds" will have you living a life that isn't of your making.

Any *should* you pick up is a venomous, deadly poison. You're comparing yourself to an imaginary you who is not even your creation, even if it was your idea. Check yourself to be sure you're not following someone else's program.

Fear

At a basic level, fear exists to protect us from danger—real danger, such as physical harm or death. Any "danger" less than these comes to us through the air. Because fear is such a primal instinct in humans, buried in our evolutionary wiring, it travels through our systems faster than any other feeling, and at its peak, fear is the strongest of all feelings.

Fear of life-threatening situations and possible bodily harm is natural. Fear of anything else—such as negative opinions, failure, succeeding, not being enough, what others may be thinking or saying—is a learned behavior, picked up out of an adverse response to a similar situation in your past. You will unlearn that fear by the end of this book.

What "They" Say

"They" is the assumed general consensus of what people say about anything. "They" are the source of all opinions, "shoulds," and fears.

Instincts

You were born with instincts. Anything you do without needing to think is instinctive. Instincts can be drilled into you, and once something is instinctive, thinking just gets in the way. Instincts communicate much quicker than conscious thought.

Instinct is how pro athletes improvise moves and make split-second decisions in the heat of competition. In *The 33 Strategies of War*, author Robert Greene refers to a war general's instinctual ability to know what move to make, stemming from the general's deep experience, as "fingertip feel."

The pro plays off of instinct, seeing, deciding, and reacting instantaneously. The amateur needs to see, then think, then decide—and by then, the opportunity is gone. In professional sports, a split second is the difference between winning and losing. In the men's 100-meter dash final at the 2016 Olympics, the difference between first place (the gold medal winner) and tenth place was 0.25 seconds. That's not enough time to observe, contemplate, decide, and then act.

Your instincts speak at the volume of a whisper. In contrast, through-the-air material is loud and obnoxious. Depending on how long it's been since you've accessed your instincts, your instincts may have decided it isn't worth the effort to even try talking to you. When a prevalent through-the-air idea clashes with instinct, instinct is not only at a decibel disadvantage, but it can also be rusty and unsure of itself. It's your job to rebuild its confidence.

Everyone is sure of their own opinions when they don't have to live with the fallout of following those opinions. Conversely, almost everyone is unsure of their instincts, having had them crowded out and shouted down for so long that we can't even remember what they sound like.

That small voice in your head is never wrong, and it will never mislead you. Make contact with it, and prove that its voice will be heard and heeded.

Destiny

What were you put on this earth for? What were you meant to do? You may not know exactly what right now. What you can do is use the process of elimination to know what's *not* for you, if nothing else.

Your destiny is the very reason for your existence, and it comes from deep in your soul. To get in touch with what's going on there, anything through the air must be quieted down or removed.

What *You* Say

Other people will always have something to offer, even if they're not saying it directly to you (for example, a YouTube video or a tweet is meant for anyone who'll pay attention to it). Simple reason: There are more "other people" (billions of them, in fact) than the just one you. Therefore, make a conscious choice that what *you* say receives high priority over what "they" say.

They've had their say, offered their opinions, and told you what you should do. Now, what do *you* say?

If it hasn't already happened for you, there will come a day or days when no one else believes what you believe. Others don't see the future that you see. They don't have the vision that you have. Feeling as if they're offering you much-needed advice, people will urge you to listen to the airwaves, to quit, to lower your ambitions, to not expect so much from yourself. To take it easy. To not work too hard.

Sometimes in life, you have to trust the one voice that sounds different, the voice that is pitch-perfect to you but inaudible to others: the voice traveling through the bones. Through *your* bones.

5

WHAT ARE YOU AFRAID OF?

Building confidence involves not only believing in yourself, which I covered in Chapter 3, and overcoming self-consciousness and performance anxiety, covered in Chapter 4. It also requires you to overcome your fear of success—which I'll discuss in this chapter.

WHY WOULD ANYONE FEAR SUCCESS? (AND WHAT TO DO ABOUT IT)

The fear of coming up short, even after giving our best effort, causes us to shrink and unconsciously hold back out of fear that our full game wouldn't be enough. The existence of a fear of failure eventually creates the exact failure we fear. Maybe you don't have that problem—but you're still not getting all of your game out there. Could you be unconsciously afraid that you might actually *succeed*?

What does that even mean, though? Success is what you *want*. Why would anyone be *afraid* of it?

People don't fear the actual act of obtaining success. What they fear is everything that comes with success.

Fear of Public Opinion

If you create enough success, you create a new problem: attention. People you don't even know begin to criticize you and your actions. Win big enough or for long enough, and people notice. Watching successful people do what they do is an industry in itself. There are entire magazines filled with photos of famous people doing essentially nothing. Some people, unconsciously fearing this by-product of success, sabotage themselves to avoid the attention.

But why the negative scrutiny? It's because of rationalization.

When you're so far above the level of other people (at least, as far as they see it), people will seek or create reasons why you're not as great as you seem. They do this so they can feel better about themselves and their own positions. Yes, some people could just as well work on their own games and feel better that way, but that takes time and effort. Finding the flaws in *your* game is much easier and faster.

Humans have master-level rationalization skills. Looking up at someone who's doing better than we are is uncomfortable: our necks start hurting, like when you sit too close to the screen at the movies. As a result, people may feel you need to be brought back to eye level. And while they look at you, seeing the highlights of your life while living through 24 hours of their own behind-the-scenes lives, they need to know that you're not so perfect. So they'll find or even create what's wrong with you to ease their own insecurities.

When people you don't know and have never met criticize you, it's not personal (though it may seem that way). They're doing what human beings do. Making the great seem not-so-great is the only way some people can sleep at night.

What can you do about it?

Accept judgment as part of the game. If you're going to step on the stage, people are going to watch. And if you do anything in front of enough people, someone is going to have something to say about it or you or both. That's the game you're signing up for.

Be happy when someone disagrees with you. As long as you're not breaking the law or hurting anyone with your actions, having anyone disagree with you is good news: it means you're standing for something. We all like feeling a part of something that not everyone can be a part of or even wants to be a part of. For every detractor you create, you'll have at least one more hardcore fan.

Unwillingness to Do What It Takes to Succeed Again

Success comes with the expectation to do it again. If you've ever worked really hard to achieve a big goal, you may have come to find that it was a lot harder than you thought it would be. When people reach success and realize exactly what it really took to get there, some make the decision to not push themselves that hard again. It's not because they're incapable, of course. It's because they are unwilling to fully engage their will.

For example, I got into a real zone one morning while training for the 2017 Miami Marathon. I was running 10 miles on this day, and for the last half of the run I moved at a speed I had never run at before for that long of a distance. During the last 25 minutes of my run, my mind took over; my body didn't feel a thing.

I finished the run and was blown away by the time I made, both in total and per mile. The first thing I thought to myself was, *now I know what I'm capable of.* The next thought was, *am I willing to push myself to that limit again?*

Notice I said *willing* to push myself, not *able* to push myself. I had just proven that I was able. To know that we're capable of doing something, we need only one example of having done it. *Will*, on the other hand—the choice to achieve that performance— is another story. Again, it wasn't my body feeling great that made that record run time happen. It was the zone I was in mentally, which any of us can get into at any time with the right tools.

Your most treasured successes took more work and more time than you expected. The next time, unlike the first, you know exactly what it takes to get there. Many people just don't want to commit to going through it again. And as you reach higher levels of achievement, skills alone become *less* important.

Every time you succeed, sustaining and repeating that success gets that much harder. Knowing this, some people opt out of the game.

Here's exactly what you can do when dealing with the "do it again" expectation:

A great performance is the standard, not the exception. The difference between a professional and an amateur is usually not a large skill difference, but a difference in what each expects of himself or herself. When you achieve these great results because of your exceptional efforts, don't look at it as an aberration. This is what you expect from yourself now, because you just proved that you're capable of delivering it.

Accept the mental challenge. This is not going to be easy, and isn't supposed to be. As the saying goes, if it was easy, everyone would do it. Know that you'll probably have to decide to push yourself harder mentally than you ever have before to maintain the standard you've proven yourself capable of.

What Fear of Success Looks Like

Succeeding in any way brings expectations—even if your success is in showing the potential to be better. Even if that expectation wasn't set by you, you'll be letting a lot of people down if you don't come through.

I spent my freshman year of college at Penn State Abington, a campus just outside of Philadelphia. I frequented the gym at Abington all summer, utilizing the otherwise empty basketball court and weight room to enhance my game. I was on campus every day that summer, and I wasn't even taking summer classes.

One morning I drove to the Abington campus without eating breakfast. I walked across campus to the cafeteria where a man I'd never seen before approached me and started talking basketball, asking me what position I played and such. It turned out that this guy was the head basketball coach at Penn State Altoona, which was a level above the league Abington played in at the time. Before we were done talking, I knew I wanted to make the move to Altoona: it was a higher level of basketball. Within two weeks, I was enrolled at Altoona as a basketball team recruit.

When I arrived at Penn State Altoona in 2001 as a basketball recruit, I wasn't ready to earn my playing time on the team. I was stuck to the bench during games, and lesser players played the minutes that would have been mine, which in turn hurt the team. We had a horrible season, and the coach who had recruited me was replaced. My lack of preparedness for the demands that would be placed on me was part of the reason.

When people see the full extent of your game, you'll have teammates, bosses, coworkers, and family members planning around the expectation of you being that great on a consistent basis, even if you never *asked* them to set that bar for you. To whom much is given (or from whom much is shown), much is expected.

Now that you know why people fear success, here are the outward signs of fear of success. Be honest with yourself and check for these.

You downplay your achievements to keep expectations low. People suffering from this affliction display the bad habit of downplaying their virtues and achievements as an involuntary reaction to any compliment, good news, or winning outcome. These people immediately attack their own success with self-deprecating comments, almost as if to protect themselves from feeling too good or raising expectations about anything.

Oh, but they're being humble, you say?

Anyone who uses the humility or not-showing-off BS justifications is showing you how much he or she is afraid of the spotlight of success. What many people tout as humility is actually *fear*. What you call being humble is actually your self-defense mechanism to ensure that you do not shine too bright, stand out, or do so well that people start expecting it from you all the time.

The majority of the population is great at feigning humility, especially in a culture where standing out draws scrutiny from people who have nothing better to do. Dimming your bright colors keeps expectations low, both of yourself and of others. Humility deflects attention.

Combat this by applying what you learned in the previous section, making your achievements a normal, standard thing, not a surprise or exception. Understand and accept that the attention is a by-product of your game and performance and is part of the package that comes with self-improvement and delivering results.

You set low goals that don't require you to stretch. These are the people who won't try out for the team or interview for the job, yet mock you for not making that team or not receiving the job offer. These are the people who see doing nothing and "avoiding" failure (at least they think) as an achievement.

Contrary to popular belief, people who fear success *do* set goals. But their goals are set so low that, even when they reach them, that achievement makes little to no impact on their lives. If those people are called out for their weak goal-setting habits, their built-in defense is that they *did set* goals, *and* they were "successful" in achieving them. Who can argue with that?

Your long-term goals, when you achieve them, should be life-altering—literally: reaching those goals should change your life in a significant way. Just making a serious pursuit of the goal, you need to change in a significant way. Any long-term goal that doesn't change you or your life significantly is not an ambitious-enough goal.

You set ambitious goals—and quit at first resistance. This is another go-to move of the success-fearing person: set goals that are super-high and ambitious (which draws admiration), give somewhat of an effort, then abruptly quit when it "doesn't work."

This is the person who wants to lose weight, and does . . . only to gain it all back the next month. Or the athlete who wants to play in the NFL, but quits football when he fails to make the varsity team as a high-school freshman.

Ambitious goals, by design, are not easy to reach and to some, they may not be easy to understand either. Ambition requires a heavy time and energy investment that may take a while to produce a return.

Here's how to get comfortable setting bigger goals:

Be honest about who and what you want to be. If you know there was no chance of being judged or ridiculed or challenged, how would you answer the questions of who you want to be? What are your true ambitions?

Know that making a real difference comes from trying something that hasn't been done. Your goals should not only change you, but also change the environment you're in and the lives of the people affected by your goals. If your biggest goal is to do something that's already been done, even if you achieve it, why would it be remembered?

Accept that you'll spend a lot of time having not yet achieved your goals. And that's OK! When you're aiming to do something that doesn't exist, there will be trial and error. There will be failure. There will be times when you scrap everything and start all over. Know that this will happen before you begin, and stick to the script you've written for yourself.

EXAMINE YOUR GAME

If you haven't failed, you're a failure. Ask yourself: *How compelling are my goals? If I achieved all of them today, would that make a noticeable difference in my life?*

TAKE IT TOO FAR

Once you understand and apply all of this, you may be wondering how you can control your confidence. *How do I control all of this confidence, Dre? Confidence is good, but I don't want to take it too far, do I?*

Yes. You *do* want to take your confidence too far—so far, in fact, that it makes people uncomfortable. You'll know it when they start putting labels on you, labels such as *Cocky, Arrogant,* and *Full of Yourself.* They'll preach humility, and try to explain why you need to let some helium out of that balloon of yours.

If you follow everything I've shared in this chapter, these people will make themselves known. The rest of this chapter is your vaccine for these losers.

Belief *Always* = Achievements

Basketball great Larry Bird once joked that when he came to the NBA, his goal was to make one million dollars. He added that his friend Magic Johnson's goal was to make 100 million dollars. The happy ending, Larry quipped, was that they both achieved their goal.

When I was 16 and still not on my high school's basketball team, I played for the local 16-and-under rec team at Finley Playground in my Mount Airy neighborhood. I was a solid, yet unspectacular contributor for the first couple games of the season before Finley hosted a Christmas tournament for our age group.

We failed to hold down our home court and were eliminated before the finals of the event. Leaving the locker room after our loss, I joked to a teammate that we lost only because *I* hadn't been getting the ball enough.

The locker room was right next to the coaches' office, and one of them heard what I had said. "What'd you say, Dre?" one of the coaches from another team asked.

I repeated myself and said, "I said, we lost because they didn't give me the ball."

I knew the coach only asked me to repeat myself because he wanted to see how firmly I would stand on my words. When I unflinchingly repeated myself, the coach didn't say anything, he just looked at me. I didn't say anything either. I just turned and walked home.

Coaches talk amongst themselves.

About a week later, our 16-and-under club reconvened for practice for the remainder of our season. My coach pulled me aside before practice.

"Dre, you talk a lot about what you can do, so I'm gonna give you a chance to prove it. We're gonna get you the ball and see what you can really do."

That conversation, and the rest of my season with that team, was a huge breakthrough for me in basketball.

The team actually ran plays designed for me to shoot—and I *made* the shots! Opposing teams came into games planning to stop *me*. My team depended on me to deliver, and most of the time, I did.

I made my high school varsity the following fall, and even though I did very little by way of performance that season, my lack of on-court achievement for that season didn't really matter because my 16-and-under performance showed me that I had the game to play college ball and the proof to back up my talk.

The saying goes, *what the mind can conceive and believe, the mind can achieve.* While conceiving and believing don't guarantee success, they set the bar for you. Your level of belief is the concrete ceiling on your achievement.

The more self-belief you have, the more things you will try. And, the more you try, the higher your chances are of achieving. To *believe* means to accept as real and as possible. Do you accept yourself? Do you see your goals as real possibilities for yourself? If you're having a hard time seeing it, think of your most cherished life achievement. I bet not everyone thought you could do it. Some may have even told you so or encouraged you to give it up. When left to be your own inspiration, you found it in you to pull that energy out of you and you made it happen. All this is proof that it can be done. This is hard evidence that belief is within your capacity.

Have the Humility to Do the Work That Allows Cockiness

Even if you don't follow boxing, you've heard of Floyd Mayweather Jr. Floyd talks a big game, and he earns a lot of money from his game because he went undefeated in his boxing career.

Floyd's detractors (and despite his record of success, there are many) would say Floyd is cocky and arrogant, among other things. I'm a Mayweather fan and I want to see him win, but on this point, I agree with his detractors: Floyd *is* Cocky and Arrogant.

However, in his defense, Floyd has positioned himself to be those things. And it's not just his fight record. For Floyd, winning a boxing match is the icing on a cake that has already been baked. If you've watched any of the HBO and Showtime documentaries that follow Floyd before his title fights, you know something: for all his braggadocio and showing off of his lifestyle, Mayweather seemed to always find ample time to get in the gym and train, often multiple times per day.

Beware of Average People Who Urge You to Stay Small

I spent my senior year of college not even on the basketball team. I'd been dismissed from the team by a new coach, a guy who hadn't recruited me. Though I still had high hopes for my basketball future, the present didn't look too promising.

I remember talking to some of the campus faculty who I'd often see in the athletic building. They knew I had been on the team the previous year, and would ask me what my plans were, now that I was graduating soon. I also remember looking at their faces when I told them my next step was to play professional basketball.

Here I was, a senior who wasn't even on the team at a D3 school, saying I was going to go pro in basketball. There was no solid proof on my track record that this would come to fruition, and the reality of my situation said there was no way. While no one openly discouraged or talked down on my professional goal, I could tell that they didn't believe me. I think most of the faculty at Penn State Altoona who knew me expected me to do what the rest of my classmates would do: get a safe job related to my degree at some company and live happily ever after.

But I had bigger plans.

Arrogance is having or showing an exaggerated estimate of one's own importance—but "exaggerated" is relative. The perfect amount for me may be too much to you, which is how such terms as *cocky* and *arrogant* exist. They are used only by people who see your confidence level as too high *for them* to ever get to—which, logic tells them, must mean there's something wrong with *you*. If your confidence were within their reach, you wouldn't be "cocky."

The small-thinking people who want you to be humble are using a different type of "humble" than what I described about Floyd Mayweather. These are not the people who are out doing the work required to keep their confidence up. These are people who are tiptoeing through life, making sure not to rustle any leaves, just to arrive safely and quietly at death.

They're the ones who tell you, no matter how good you are, to never toot your own horn or feel too good about yourself. *You can achieve everything you want if you remain level-headed and humble*, some say—by not making too much noise, not being too prideful or doing anything that would make anyone feel that you believe you are better than them (which you can't control anyway). Follow their advice, and everything will come to you.

Success, winning, and achievement are not house-trained Pomeranians. They don't come to you. They must be taken by force. Taken by people who understand that their performance is a reflection of their self-belief.

The people urging you to be humble—who are people of low importance—are not out to hurt or slow you down, at least not on purpose. They're telling you the same thing they've been telling themselves: *don't think of yourself or your work as important*. Why? Because importance draws attention, expectation, and responsibility. Those scare people.

Don't Be Shy About People Knowing How Good You Are

Letting the world know what you've done, what you're doing, and what you're about to do doesn't make you arrogant. It means you're participating in a billion-dollar industry called the news.

For example, since building my brand in 2005, I've always been proactive in getting my name and value out there. I send cold e-mails to podcasts, radio shows, blogs, and conferences offering myself as someone who can add to the conversation and help their audience. I've never been shy about people knowing my skill level—if anything, I feel I need more people to know about me!

Too many of us are too shy and tentative about tooting our own horns, but if you think about it, telling people what you're doing is an industry in itself. The people who do it best become celebrities or influencers.

Every single day in the United States, 56 million newspapers are still printed, not to mention the 440 million blogs in existence (by one report's estimate).* Why? To inform us of what other people did, are doing, or will do (or at least claim they will do). People update and polish their résumés every day to better present themselves for career opportunities. Social media's very existence depends on people's willingness to share news—or what we deem to be news—with the world. People are paid full-time salaries to uncover and report on the who, what, when, where, why, and how of life.

When you become great at what you do, it's your duty to let the world know about it. Be great enough for long enough, and the news industry may start telling your business without ever asking if it's OK. And look, all of life is a business. My simple definition for business is the exchange of resources between people. Usually, the medium of exchange is money. Food isn't free. Neither are your clothes, your home, or your mode of transportation. The electricity that keeps your lights on and the bed you sleep in all cost money.

---

* "How Many Blogs Are There in the World?" http://mediakix.com/2017/09/how-many-blogs-are-there-in-the-world/#gs.PY_b4og.

Before money comes into the conversation, though, you need people's' attention, time, focus, and energy, which they'll happily give you if you have information they need. From there, if everything checks out, *then* you get the money. This is selling—and when you inform people of how good you are at what you do, you're selling them on paying attention. You sell people every day on liking you, trusting you, listening to you, agreeing with you, and following you.

EXAMINE YOUR GAME

Making your credentials known isn't arrogant; it's business. And as all of life is a business. Sharing your news is more than part of your work. It's life.

Don't Forget What Got You There: The Work

Never forget what put you in position to be here: your effort and discipline. As soon as you stop giving those, your license to be cocky is revoked. How could you bring yourself to feel important when you know you haven't been doing the work to earn that feeling? And if you *are* going to work every single day, who is anyone to tell you that you don't deserve to be important?

The most arrogant people you can think of have been that way (at least from your perspective) for a long time. The only way to stay that way, and keep earning people's attention, is to produce. If someone is cocky yet isn't producing results, people stop paying attention.

• • •

As we've seen in this chapter and the previous two, confidence is what gets you out there boldly and authentically. However, even with all your confidence, we are not perfect: things don't always go exactly as we planned.

What do you do then, when you've been sticking to the disciplines, believing in yourself and doing everything right—and things are still not working for you?

You become Mentally Tough.

That's my WOYG Principle #3, and I'll tell you all about it in the next chapter.

6

MENTAL TOUGHNESS

The larger and more ambitious your goals, the rougher things will be on your way there. Simply stated, Mental Toughness is the measure of how much Confidence and Discipline you can muster and/or maintain when things get rough. Mental toughness is the capacity to continue showing up and doing the work and putting yourself out there, even when the success you planned for has yet to show up to meet you, and it didn't even call to tell you it would be late. Developing Mental Toughness is WOYG Principle #3, and this chapter describes how to do exactly that.

• • •

It's inevitable that, somewhere along the line, things won't go the way you planned—maybe one of those things will be the one thing you thought you could depend on.

One day, I was practicing with my team at Penn State Altoona. I had just grabbed a defensive rebound and started dribbling up court, the transition situation I thrived in as a basketball player due to my ball-handling skill and athleticism. Since I was more athletic than any of my teammates, I knew I could score an easy basket. The coach's whistle interrupted my personal fast break. Coach Armen Gilliam was a 13-year NBA veteran who had become a college basketball coach, and everyone turned to see what he wanted.

"Dre! You need to give the ball to our guards! I've told you this before! No wonder you're leading the team in turnovers!"

Silence.

"See, this is why we're losing games. We're all trying to do things as a team, but *Dre* wants to do things *his* way."

Though this particular tirade was directed at me, this was Gilliam's go-to method of coaching: catch someone making a mistake, then frame this mistake as the overarching reason for the team's struggles. I was thick-skinned enough to handle it, but Gilliam's scolding had ridden a few players to tears or to quit the basketball team completely.

All the players on this team had seen this movie many times before; today was merely my turn as the star. I attempted to brush it off so we could continue our scrimmage. "All right, man, all right. Play ball."

"No! No! Everyone, bring it in."

We gathered around for Gilliam to deliver what became the death blow to my college basketball career.

"You know, over the holidays, I was hanging with Bobby Knight . . ."

Bobby Knight is a famous former college basketball coach from the University of Indiana, known for his drill-sergeant-like dictatorship style in dealing with players and even game officials. Knight was nicknamed "The General." Many college coaches looked up to Knight as a shining example of how to coach a team through fear, intimidation, and a never-question-me attitude. Kenny Macklin, my previous coach at Altoona (Gilliam had replaced Macklin) even had a photo of himself with Bobby Knight hanging in his office.

Gilliam continued, ". . . and Bobby Knight had a sign up in his office that said, 'This is Not Burger King: You Cannot Have It Your Way.' Dre, you cannot have it your way. Thank you for your time today." With that, he motioned to the brown double doors leading out of the gym.

I walked out of Adler Gymnasium in a state of shock. Gilliam had been doing player-bashing rants all season, but he hadn't kicked anyone out of practice, or done anything other than yell. Maybe that damned Bobby Knight had given him the idea of what to do with me. I drove back to my off-campus apartment, wondering what the hell I was going to do with my college life now, since I was probably done with college basketball. I didn't have the résumé to facilitate a transfer to another school's team, and I could read the writing on the wall of what the new coach was doing with the program: clearing out the old (read: players like me) and bringing in the new (read: players he'd chosen himself).

Up until that day in January 2003, my goal was to make it to pro basketball. I had scarce resources—no connections, no game film (as proof of my skill), no tangible reasons to believe it would happen, no real plans, no role models as proof someone could make it from Division 3 or Altoona, and no support.

When the basketball team played its next game without me, the reality of my hoops career hit me: I was now nowhere, playing for no one. Over the next two-and-a-half years, I would be forced to rebuild my basketball life.

In college, I now didn't have a team to practice with, or trainers or coaches to work with. I was forced to make up a training schedule that fit around both my classes and the basketball team's schedule so I could use the gym when the team wasn't around and still work on my game during my senior year (at the time, our campus had only one gym).

After I graduated college, my job replaced going to classes, and I didn't have the convenience of a close-by gym. So I wound up practicing on the same outdoor courts I'd grown up on until the weather got too cold, and then I joined a local LA Fitness gym.

From the outside looking in at that point, there was nothing different about me from the many older guys I had grown up playing against at Finley. I was out of school, and playing basketball for fun whenever I could find the time. I realized I was living the exact life I had been aiming to avoid. To the outside world, I was a former college basketball player who was out of the game, and nothing else. I was in my early twenties, not getting any younger, and had no prospects for making a career happen. My goal was looking less and less probable by the day.

But none of that stopped me from trying. I continued to work on my game while keeping my eyes and ears open for any chance to get myself seen and start my professional basketball career.

● ● ●

My professional basketball career finally began in the fall of 2005, after two-plus years of not being on an organized team and a postgrad year not having many solid prospects. Nothing in my reality said that my hopes would come true, yet I had to continue doing the work and believing in a result that hadn't yet come to life. That, along with my debut on a little-known video site that had started that same year, created a following of people who not only admired the way I played, but saw a lot of themselves in my story.

DECIDE WHETHER YOU WILL BE A STORY OR A STATISTIC

Years ago, the NCAA had a long-running commercial that featured student-athletes working out, playing their sports, in the classroom, and finally in business clothing working at their (future) jobs. The voice-over through the video shared that the NCAA had thousands of student-athletes, most of whom would be going pro in something *other* than sports.

The commercial was accurate. Most of my college team-mates didn't need a commercial to know their futures would be in something other than sports. And, unlike the "revenue sports" of football and basketball, most college sports' professional equivalents didn't have structured leagues offering better money than a "regular" job anyhow.

When it comes to goal setting and self-improvement, you will hear people like me stressing that you get clear on your outcomes:

- What do you want?
- If you have difficulty articulating what you want, try flipping the question around: what do you *not* want?
- What would be the worst outcome? (If you can't quite figure out a goal, the anti-goal, so to speak, can help you eliminate possibilities, and you can use the opposite of the anti- to find what you do want.)

In my case, I knew I didn't want to walk through the glass doors of the fictional companies in the NCAA ad. More important, I've always hated being lumped in with everyone else, like "most" of the NCAA's student-athletes. The commercial made me want to defy the statistic.

To me, the NCAA's commercial was really aimed toward the fringe pro, the player who is almost good enough but *not quite*. The player who would get close enough to almost taste success—so close that he would be deluded into repeatedly trying. This player was the one who would need the most help and the message in that commercial. Meanwhile, I was a player at an NCAA D3 school who was not even on the damned team; I wasn't even worth the ad spend. But, luckily for me, I'd always been a bit delusional when it came to basketball. Sitting the bench as a high school senior and being kicked off the college team didn't bode well for me. To be recruited just one year later was a pipe dream. And to expect to play pro after not even playing my last year-and-a-half of D3 college ball was too ridiculous even for a movie script.

• • •

If you've ever had a goal that was big, ambitious, or otherwise out of the ordinary relative to where you were, maybe you had someone share the statistics of your goal with you, like these:

- Only one in a million basketball players ever goes pro.
- TV networks only green-light one of every 300 shows pitched to them.
- Most books published never earn back their advances.

Some statistics are shared with the intention to discourage you. Sometimes, though, people are genuinely trying to help or motivate you by letting you know just how rare and unlikely your desired outcome is. Most people who start with big goals become contributors to the numbers, another of the millions who dreamed, tried, thought, and planned but ultimately did not get what they started after. These people are the Statistics.

The tiny few remaining are the Stories.

The Story people aren't special—at least, not on the surface. They go through the same things the Statistics deal with. Not making a team. Passed up for a big promotion. Lack of familial support. Open hostility and discouragement. General bad luck.

The difference is, despite the challenges, setbacks, and bad fortune, the Stories keep going and persevere at every point along the way where the Statistics fall off. Then these winners—who are the literal authors of history—share their journeys with the public. The Statistics don't get to say much, because people don't pay money or attention to hear from losers.

Know this: if your glory was never in jeopardy, there would be no story. Without a moment where it looks as if it's surely over for you, there's no value in the achievement for you or anyone else. What can you offer to help the challenges the next person faces?

I want to know that the person speaking on stage or writing a book has been where I am. That's how I know they're speaking to me.

EXAMINE YOUR GAME

Perseverance makes your Story relevant.
Quitting just makes you another Statistic who gave up.

If you have a goal, you're going to go through the fire while you're going after that goal, whether or not you achieve it. You'll have to go through whether you give up or keep going. So you might as well make a Story out of it.

Easy for me to say, right? It all sounds good until you're in the middle of the storm. What do you do when a setback really hits you in your heart, and hurts you to the core? How can you ensure that your setback is just a setup for a comeback?

COMMAS, NOT PERIODS: HOW FAR YOU GO DEPENDS ON HOW YOU HANDLE OBSTACLES

How far you go in anything is not about *if* you face setbacks or *if* you're ever counted out. It's about how many of those would-be *periods* you turn into *commas*.

In writing, a period indicates the completion of a thought. A comma indicates a pause in a thought, just before more is added. The comma indicates the thought is not complete. Although I suppose many people would like to turn periods into commas, I suspect many people just don't know how to.

For almost everything that happens in life, you have a choice of a comma or a period. Quitting is a period. Doing nothing is a period. If you aren't fully committed to overcoming a setback to get to your goal, that's a period.

Right now you may be thinking, every situation is unique. It's not so easy to put a comma after some outcomes. I agree. There's nothing in *Work On Your Game* that says anything about "easy." Putting commas after setbacks has only one requirement: to make every unpleasant outcome a mere footnote in the full story of you, to do one thing, and one thing only.

EXAMINE YOUR GAME

Give a damn.
Choose a goal or destination that you care about
enough to pursue, even when it's not easy.

Here's the five-step process to turning every would-be period into a comma on your success journey.

Step 1: Ask Yourself, *What Can I Learn from This?*

When we win, we celebrate. When we lose, we contemplate.

There's a lesson in everything. When bad stuff happens, after getting over the shock and sadness, ask yourself:

- *What can I learn from this?*
- *What did I not know before that I know now?*
- *What new knowledge did I gain that will serve me in the future?*

These questions are easy to write, but hard to call on while in the depths of despair. That's why you condition your mind to ask the questions without conscious input, as I described in Chapter 1 on Mental Conditioning.

Step 2: Ask Yourself, *How Can I Improve as a Person Because of This?*

When we lose, we think of how bad it is, how mad we are, and what could have been. The challenge is how quickly you can get to asking yourself:

- *What about the experience will make me better in the future?*
- *What value did I gain as a person that I can take with me to the next thing in life?*
- *Why am I better now than I was before?*

Step 3: Ask Yourself, *Who Has Been Through This and Survived, and What Can I Learn from That Person's Experience?*

The great thing about our world having so many people and so many ways to share our lives is that you're probably not the first person to go through what you're going through. Look around enough, and you're bound to find someone who has seen the exact path you're currently on and would be happy to tell you what he or she knows.

Step 4: Ask Yourself, *What's the Next Thing I Can Do to Capitalize on This Situation?*

What happened is messed up, we know. But it's over. Life will go on, with or without you. Ask yourself:

- *What am I going to do next?*
- *Where's the opportunity in my circumstance?*
- *If I had to find one, what would it be?*
- *What's the best thing about where I am now?*
- *If I were really happy about this, why would that be?*

Step 5: Ask Yourself, *Why Is the Game NOT Over?*

This is the billion-dollar, comma-creating question. This question opens space for you to find a reason to continue. If left unanswered, this question mark slowly melts into a period. So ask yourself the following questions:

- *What do I have to do that I still haven't done?*
- *What do I need to do to prove to myself?*
- *What potential have I not yet fulfilled?*

Stuff will happen that is out of your control. What you do control is how long you stay there before you move on to complete the rest of your life. Sit still for too long, and you become a period, an ending.

But how do you know when you've tried enough? How can you gauge when it's time to give up on a quest and when you need to try one more time?

Until Is the Essence of Persistence

Until is the key word in the Mental Toughness dictionary. *Until* is your word when you're fully committed to an outcome. *Until* is the mindset of a person who is willing to sell himself out to a cause due to his intense belief in that cause. It's the word in the mind of someone getting up to go at it again even though yesterday sucked. *Until* is your word of defiance when everyone has thrown the facts in your face and told you to give it up.

Until is your word as you dial one more number to solicit donations, knowing someone is going to answer this time. It's the word you'll say to yourself after you're turned down, ignored, or declined—again. I became familiar with *until* when I was sending more than 700 personalized e-mails to pro basketball teams hoping to reengage my career—and it worked!

Until is the word of the person who sees success as the only possibility, as opposed to those who have an "if" or "when" mentality—people who say things like this:

- *I'll keep doing this IF it works out.*
- *I'll commit WHEN I can be sure it's working out.*
- *I'll invest in myself WHEN I start generating revenue.*
- *I know I need help, and I'll hire help IF it doesn't cost too much.*
- *This is a good idea . . . IF it works out.*
- *I'll hold myself accountable WHEN I get back on track.*

Some people, because of circumstances, have an *Until* mindset by default. Parents are a good example. They care for their child *until* the child can fend for themselves. Fund-raisers call for donations *until* they raise their goal amount. Leaders like Mahatma Gandhi, Martin Luther King Jr., Malcolm X, and Mother Teresa preached their message not *if* people would listen and not *when* it was convenient. They did their work and spread their gospel *until* they couldn't, inspiring millions of people, some of whom weren't even alive during their time.

Until is a mindset you won't fully grasp *until* the next time you need it. But if you think into your past, you already know what it feels like.

EXAMINE YOUR GAME

Think of a time when your back was to the wall.
Something needed to happen, and it needed
to happen right then. What happened?

A sense of urgency flooded your senses. A rush of energy sharpened your focus, opened your gates of creativity, and moved you to immediate action, even if you had just thought you didn't have any more push in you. If an action did not produce the result, you immediately moved to the next possibility, wasting no time complaining or deliberating. If your phone wasn't ringing, you rang phones and knocked on doors. You were committed to taking action *until* you got what you wanted, and miraculously, you received it.

EXAMINE YOUR GAME

Accept that there's no magic formula. When is the
last time you were all-in on something, and why did
you feel that way? The answers are clues to your
inner drive, and the key to reactivating yourself.

CHECK YOUR BAD BREATH: FIND SOMEONE TO TELL YOU THE TRUTH ABOUT HOW YOU'RE DOING

There's a story about a high-ranking diplomat who was told he had bad breath by a rival minister. Arriving home that evening, the diplomat confronted his wife, asking her why she had never told him his breath was bad. The diplomat's wife replied that she had assumed all men's breath smelled the same way as her husband's, so she didn't think anything was amiss.

The diplomat didn't have anyone around him to tell him the truth. The problem for many people is that they don't *want* to hear the truth, no matter how much they need it. The "uncoachable" label is smacked on any athlete who bristles at being told, metaphorically, how bad his breath is. The uncoachable player runs any feedback through his filters of "How do I feel about what you said or how you said it?" rather than "Will this help me improve?"

Former NBA coach Phil Jackson has discussed his experiences with Kobe Bryant after Bryant's game and skills expanded and he became become somewhat "uncoachable." Kobe wanted to explore more of his potential, and this tended to conflict with the aims of the team. Kobe believed he could do more than what Jackson was asking of him and bristled at Jackson's attempts to, as Kobe said, "rein [him] in."

Any pro athlete has to deal with some tough coaches or trainers along the way. That coach who yells at you twice as often as he yells at everyone else combined. The trainer who never seems satisfied with your efforts. The coach who sees the stats you put up and how easy you make it look as though they mean you're not working hard enough.

For example, during my freshman year of college, my coach had a talk with me before the season about the fact that while I was performing well, it was obvious that I could do more if I played harder. My 18-year-old brain didn't understand what the problem was. I thought I was one of the better players and was able to be that while giving less than my best effort. Where was the problem in that? This wound up being a season-long issue between myself and my coach.

FORGET ABOUT WHAT OTHERS THINK OF YOU

I was listening to a recorded lecture given by Napoleon Hill, author of *Think and Grow Rich*, one of the bestselling business books of all time. In it, Hill advises his students to push against the habit of worrying about what "they" will say. Hill admits that though he has looked far and wide, he has yet to identify who "they" are.*

I mentioned this problem briefly in Chapter 4, in the section called "What 'They' Say," but I want to address it in more detail here. In 2015, hip-hop artist DJ Khaled solved the mystery with his popular phrase, "Stay away from they." Khaled referred to the naysayers, haters, and anyone else trying to undermine your success in any way.

We all try to pretend we don't care what other people think of us. We're self-conscious about being successful, among so many who are not successful. We're embarrassed to fail publicly. The unconscious discomfort leads to self-destructive behaviors that undo the success we are working so hard for.

---

* https://itunes.apple.com/us/album/napoleon-hill-in-his-own-voice/668322814.

There are times when we *should* care what other people think of us. Job interviews, dates, political campaigns, publishing, and live performances are good examples. If the people watching don't like you or don't want more from you, what they think matters a lot. However, we apply this need-their-approval mindset to parts of our lives where outside opinion isn't important.

The following two internal strategies will ensure you don't fall into the what-will-they-say trap, or help you climb out if you've fallen in it.

Strategy #1: Keep in Mind That No One Is Thinking About You

Despite your strong confirmation bias, most people, most of the time, are not thinking about you or judging you at all. Other people aren't even thinking of you while they're looking at or talking to and about you. Yes, it's true. In those cases, they're talking and thinking about themselves, merely using you as a convenient projection screen.

Often when you look at other people, you're not really looking *at* them; you're comparing what you see in them to what you see in yourself or what you've seen in others who are similar. If you do any public speaking or performance, you've looked into the audience and seen blank faces looking back at you. Those people may be judging you, but not in a negative way. They're thinking about how what you're saying or doing applies to *them*. They are using you to think about themselves. We all do this, all the time.

When other people see you, you're a reflection of their beliefs, insecurities, pride, areas for improvement, and anything else they have trouble seeing in themselves. Don't concern yourself with how other people are judging you. Because even when they are, they're really not.

When I speak on stages, I'm not concerned with what the audience thinks of me. I've already been hired to be there; what the audience is evaluating is how what I'm saying applies to them—which then affects their opinion of me. It's what they see for themselves that formulates that opinion.

Strategy #2: Recognize That the Only Thing That Works Is *People*

By age 16, I was tired of kids mocking me for not being able to dunk. I decided I would train myself to dunk a basketball.

I read an ad in *SLAM* magazine for a program that guaranteed to increase my vertical jump by 8 to 12 inches in 15 weeks of training. I mailed a money order to the address in the ad (welcome to the nineties!). The 20-page instructional booklet came a few weeks later, and I got to work.

Halfway through the 15 weeks, results were showing. I was jumping higher and more quickly. My speed and lateral movements were more explosive. By the end of summer 1998, I could dunk easily, opening up a new facet of my game.

I repeated that 15-week vertical jump program again in college and twice more in my professional years. Players I played with would sometimes ask me what I did to train my athletic ability. I gave them my copy of the program to use on their own.

What happened for them? Well, nothing happened. None of those players achieved results, for good reason: none even *completed* the required 15 weeks. One player said it was too much work. Another said while he could see it had worked for me, it just didn't work *for him*. Others quietly quit the program and never mentioned it to me again.

This experience taught me two things about myself and other people:

1. Most people never finish what they start. Which meant if I could develop a habit of *completing* things, I could get ahead, regardless of my resources or talent.
2. Many people "try" things, with no belief in a positive result. The players I gave the vertical jump program to had doubts and negative expectations from the beginning. Therefore, they didn't bring their full selves to the training, and subsequently, the weakest pretexts were good enough reasons to quit.

I've published more than 6,000 basketball drills online. Sometimes players would find my stuff and, seeing me practicing alone, ask:

How can I be sure these drills and moves will work in real games? They look good when you're doing them alone—but what about when someone is trying to stop you? What if the defender is taller or faster, or more experienced? How can I be sure your stuff will really WORK?

This seems like a legitimate question, right? It makes sense to want to know that the tactics, tips, strategies, and advice you're taking will produce a result. Isn't it smart to be assured that something will actually *work* before you do it?

Yes, it makes sense—so much sense in fact, that many people never do anything.

See, people waste time seeking assurances and guarantees that something they're *thinking about* doing will produce a result. But, as the saying goes, results precede work only in the dictionary. Hence, as nothing can be guaranteed before effort is applied, many people never start.

And they have logical excuses at the ready:

- *I don't know enough yet to begin.*
- *I'm not sure this will work.*
- *I don't want to waste time on something that's not guaranteed.*
- *I want to make sure I get it right when I begin.*
- *I don't want to half-ass things.*

There's only one thing in life that works: People. Strategies don't work. Tips, tactics, tools, and hacks don't work. Drills and exercises and programs and online courses don't work. *Human beings* work.

Have you ever seen two different people in the same place, employing the exact same strategy, but only one person gets the result? We can't fully blame or credit the strategy. The major variable is the people involved.

Any time you fail to take full responsibility for something, you're setting yourself up to have it never go right. What if your coworkers and teammates never improve their skills? What if your tools never get replaced or updated? If it's *their* fault, what can *you* do?

Powerful people never blame their tools, teammates, or anything outside of their full control. They are therefore empowered to make things happen. And when it turns out to be the wrong thing, the powerful make it the right thing.

• • •

I played in a recreational league at a local LA Fitness in Tampa Bay, Florida, after coming home from playing in Montenegro. I'd played pretty well in Montenegro, so my confidence was high and I physically felt great. I met a guy who was a former college player himself who asked me if I would play on a team he was putting in the league, and I agreed. But this guy played in only one game before other commitments forced him to miss the rest of the season, leaving me with a team of players who were not very good. I realized that with this team, I had only one exhausting-but-fun option: dominate the action and score all the points. While I earlier lamented my former teammate Gus's strategy of doing the exact same thing, this was a different situation: Gus had very competent teammates on his side; I did not. My decision was more strategic than selfish.

If you find that your strategy isn't working, first make sure *you* are working. Are you lazy? Are you lacking in skill? Are you holding back? Are you making weak excuses about everything? Is there anyone around you who would tell you this if it were true? Next, look at your strategy. If your plan is faulty, edit or swap your plan for a new one. If that plan doesn't work, make another plan, and another, until you find one that does work (all given that you are still working). This perpetuating rule never expires.

As a player, I never did any lower-body weight lifting. For one, I falsely believed it would slow me down, and for two, I didn't know what I was doing (proper form is of extreme importance when lifting heavy free weights). This became obvious when I tried deadlifting.

Having no idea of proper lifting form, I hurt my lower back and dealt with pain in that area for months. I didn't try any more lower-body lifts again until years later, when I learned proper form and the deadlift actually became my favorite strength exercise. It wasn't the exercise that was the issue; it was my own lack of knowledge and training.

●　●　●

Plans, strategies, and programs are just words. They don't move, talk, or exert effort. These inanimate objects *never* work.

People work. Or, they don't.

Strategy #3: Live with No Regrets

There's no worse feeling than regret. Especially the regrets of what you didn't do. The worst part about regret is that there's not much you can do about it but revel in what might have been.

You can just as easily choose not to have regrets. Whatever happened, happened. There's nothing to do about it now but live to the fullest. Let the past stay the past, and make your present so great that old regrets wash away.

Maybe you have some strong regrets, regrets that eat away at you sometimes, knowing you can't go back and change the past. In that case, you're left with two questions:

1. *What can I do about the past regrets that slow me down in the present?*
2. *How can I ensure I don't have any new regrets moving forward? How can I maximize the time I have, leaving nothing undone, unsaid, no life unlived?*

The answer to #1 is simple: It's gone, so let it go. *Amor fati* is a Latin phrase meaning "love of fate." Anything and everything that has happened in your life thus far has happened for a reason; it all contributed to you being who, what, and where you are now.

I'm sure you have been in situations where, had things gone just slightly differently, you wouldn't be where you are today. All of those situations, combined with any possible regrets, make you as you are, right now, how and where you are in life. If you were to go back and "fix" all your possible regrets, you'd also have to risk all those positive breaks, hoping they would break your way again. Would you take that bet?

Regarding the second question, about the future, here's what you'll do to ensure no regret finds you in the future:

Engage in more action, less reflection. Here's a simple truth about us: Most of the time when we don't get what we want, it's because we didn't do enough. We didn't work hard enough. Didn't ask enough. Didn't believe in ourselves enough. Didn't insist on others getting involved enough. Think about times you've come up short: Is there something could you have done more of? My ill-fated junior season of college basketball could have ended differently had I had a conversation with my coach and understood exactly what he wanted from me, instead of entering into a power struggle that I was too young and dumb to realize I could not win.

Despite this, many people have an innate fear of going "too far," of doing too much, of setting their prices too high, of over-exerting themselves and exhausting their resources. How many times in life did you fail because you did too much, went too far, overplayed your hand? Maybe you have one or two; most people I talk to cannot recall enough to need two hands. One thing I'm sure of: you have many more "not enough" regrets than you have "too much" regrets.

We don't do enough *a lot* more often than we do too much. But we have a sharper memory for things going bad than for things that worked out. When we don't do enough, we absolve ourselves of responsibility: "I didn't do anything wrong, but . . ."

When you go too far and it hurts you, you draw a direct relationship between what you did and this undesirable out-come. Therefore we have a much stronger association with—and aversion to—going what we deem "too far." Thus, we think ourselves out of winning and opportunity. When things are "good enough," we fear the forward step that sets off the bomb and blows it all up. This is all fear, an instinct we cannot and should not eliminate (because it keeps us alive) but must learn to control.

But how?

Next time you want to do something, stop wasting so much time in reflection and just damn do it. Your speed and decisiveness propels you ahead of the fearful and timid masses. You create mental and physical momentum. In business these days, as soon as I have a negative feeling about a person I'm working with, I end my relationship with him or her. While this is not always easy, I've learned that my gut is usually right and the longer I wait, the more I lose because of my hesitation.

You may wonder if this applies to one who has little knowledge or experience. Yes: although you may mess up, at least you'll know what actions produce what results. And you now have valuable experience that you can't obtain merely by planning and reading. Plus, the more action you take, the sooner and more likely you take the right actions and produce a result.

When I was on my mass–e-mailing campaign in 2007, I hadn't taken any courses on e-mail marketing or talked to any players who had gotten a contract through the same methods. I just took action and continued until something happened!

Try one of your ridiculous ideas. Some people's idea of crazy and ridiculous is to e-mail an expert asking for help. For someone else, it's jumping out of a plane. For you, it may be asking for a pay raise or striking up a conversation with a neighbor. No matter what it is, you have some ridiculous ideas that scare you to even think about.

So try it. Do something you'd never do, say what you would never say, go further than you're comfortable with. Just *once*, find out how far you can go. You'll see it wasn't as crazy as you thought—or that you're crazier than you knew yourself to be. You'll develop courage to try more things. This energy alone will kill a lot of possible regrets.

Adopt a new mindset: would I rather do it and regret it, or do nothing and regret that? Change your perspective on risk taking and what you may call *going too far*. Would you rather burn out (from doing too much, possibly running out of fuel) or rust out (from doing nothing until you're unusable)?

A regret is an open-ended question. *If I had done or said this, what would have happened? How could things have been different?* The worst part of regret is the unknown that you'll never have an answer to. So your new mindset is:

- *Would I rather try something and have it fail in the worst possible way?*
- *OR do nothing and live the rest of my life with the question of what could have been?*

Would you rather know what happens, instead of staring at a big question mark of what could have happened?

When you try and mess up, even failing miserably, you now have:

1. **A story to tell.** You went through something and came out on the other end. This is now a part of who you are—and can be used as incentive to keep pushing through the hard stuff. *Experience.* Experience separates you from those who only thought about or heard of doing what you did.
2. **Activity knowledge.** You know from experience that *this* action produces *this* result. Activity knowledge is infinitely more valuable than book knowledge.
3. **Less fear of doing it.** Fears feeds on the unknown. You've been through it; you know what happens.
4. **Momentum.** Now that you're in motion, why not try doing even more?
5. **Energy.** Activity doesn't drain energy; it creates more energy.

How many times have you done something new and messed up 100 percent of it? Never. The only way to mess up 100 percent is to not try in the first place. Through the very act of making the attempt, you're setting yourself up for success. The saying is *you can't fail until you quit*. You cannot possibly fail by starting. Do it.

Bottom line: you will have very few, maybe zero, regrets in life from the things you do. On the other hand, 99 percent of your regrets will be stuff you passed on, stopped short in, didn't take far enough, and things you didn't say.

─────────── EXAMINE YOUR GAME ───────────

You're better off regretting what you did do
than regretting what you didn't do.

Strategy #4: Remember: You Don't Have to Prove Sh*t to Anyone

Have you ever gone after a goal for any of the following reasons?

- To shut people up?
- To prove that you were right all along?
- To prove that you're good enough?

These can be really motivating reasons, and you may well get there using them. But you're not helping yourself when your efforts are aimed at proving something to other people, especially when these people are not the high achievers we truly would want to compare ourselves to. So why the need to measure up to what they think?

The people you are trying to prove things to are usually:

- Behind you in achievements.
- Ahead of you, but stagnant while you're advancing. That your progress hasn't caught up to theirs yet gives them a false feeling of superiority.
- Not trying to better themselves.
- Not genuinely happy to see you improving.
- Not willing to help you improve in any way due to their scarcity mindset.

When your motivation is to prove others wrong and shut them up, you're setting yourself up for a game you cannot win. As soon as you do what "they" say you couldn't, there will be more of them, and they'll come up with some other qualification or reasoning that renders you (a) still not where you "should" be, as the target got moved, or (b) not as good as a random third person who is further ahead.

• • •

Playing basketball on the playgrounds of Philadelphia, there are trash-talkers. Often, the biggest talkers don't play in the games. They're the spectators.

People who line the sidelines and may never play in games get their "incompetent" by trying to get a reaction or response from one of the players or a fellow spectator. It doesn't even matter to the spectator/heckler if the reaction he gets is positive or negative. Just getting the response is, for him, as close to being in the game as he'll get.

One common phrase the heckler uses is *show me somethin'!*, a phrase meant to entice a player to display some level of skill for the heretofore withheld approval of the heckler. This refrain makes it easy for the heckler to figure he's involved now: if you make a good play, the heckler could reason, you did it because of the need to indeed show him something. If you don't do anything significant, you might be crumbling under the pressure of the moment. Players on the court use this as well; playing pickup ball in Philly, you might even hear this from people *on your team*.

What it really boils down to is this: there are many people out there who would rather put the onus to perform on *you* than put the same mandate on themselves.

It's much easier to demand that others step up their game, do their job better, make more shots, play better defense, close more sales, or otherwise show something than it is for someone to demand it of himself.

The *show-me something* economy, if you will, has spawned all kinds of media. Everyone has an opinion on what someone else needs to do, and how well, how fast, and with whom the person should do it. People speak as if someone meeting their requirements validates the performer in some way. Big TV networks dedicate entire shows to talking heads who spew opinions about what someone else needs to do. During the big sporting events, people bloviate on social media about what certain players need to do at the risk of the speaker's personal scorn.

Warning: If you find yourself doing this, ever, you have temporarily become a loser. Cut it out, immediately.

The more you do, the more people who become aware of you and will have an opinion on you. There are people out there who have useful input for you; it's your job to separate the essential from the peanut gallery of many. The person making the demand for performance rarely does anything worth looking at—that's why he or she *needs* you to put on the "show"!

Leave these losers to the nothingness they deserve to dwell in. You don't have to prove or show sh*t to anyone.

Remember:

1. In being a fan of your favorite athletes and celebrities, never expect more from them than you expect from yourself. This doesn't mean you lower your expectations for the home team's upcoming season. It means . . .
2. Raise the standards of what you expect *you* to do anytime you think to expect more from someone else.
3. Imagine that your life were on TV, your every move watched and scrutinized. There's a camera on you, following your every little action, facial expression, and conversation. What would *your* fans say about you? What would be criticized, and how much of it would be accurate? How long would people watch before deciding you weren't interesting enough to pay attention to?

7

○────────────────○

GO-GETTER

Personal initiative is about being a self-starter and *making* things happen instead of waiting for them to happen. This chapter introduces WOYG Principle #4: Personal Initiative, on the importance of taking personal ownership of your own success—of doing things *before* you're told or asked to do them. Before circumstance crowds in and forces your hand. Before you see or hear someone else doing it. And before a sense of urgency is forced on you by a deadline.

▄▄▄ BE PERSISTENT: FOLLOW-UP IS A KEY ▄▄▄ FACTOR IN TAKING INITIATIVE

My first ever YouTube video featured an exhibition dunk, followed by some game highlights. The best part of the video, though, is how I even acquired the footage.

I attended a professional basketball exposure camp in June of 2005. I'd spoken to the camp's organizer on the phone weeks prior to the event to find out when I would receive the game tape from the camp. That was important, because the camp footage would be my introduction to any agents, coaches, or teams to market myself as a potential player or client.

The organizer told me I should get my camp footage within a week after the camp ended. But that week came and went, and I still didn't have my game footage. The summer was ticking away, and European pro teams started practices in August. I needed that tape.

I sent the organizer several e-mails that produced a bunch of excuses but no tape. Someone else might have given up, but I knew it was up to me to get what I needed. So I kept politely but firmly letting her know that the tape from the camp was how 99.9 percent of the basketball world would come to know me, and three days later, I received a padded envelope in the mail with my VHS tape.

—————— EXAMINE YOUR GAME ——————

Sometimes you have to start a fire where there's no fire.

BE OPEN TO ALL NEW OPPORTUNITIES

Footage from that tape introduced me to YouTube and served as the bulk of my first three-minute YouTube video on April 28, 2006. The audience's positive response to what they saw persuaded me to start taking my newly gifted camera with me to the basketball gym in 2007 to record my trainings. Those roughly-edited recordings created an audience of fans, many of whom are still with me today, along with those who came on somewhere along the way or those who stepped away from basketball but reengaged with me when they saw me talking about stuff that went further than hoops.

Between 2006 and 2010, my fans asked a lot of questions about my on-court game and experiences in basketball. My answers—all on video—grabbed people's attention and spawned more questions. *Wait! How did you go from barely playing in high school to walking on in college to the pros? What was your mindset? How do you stay confident? How do you deal with nerves before the games?*

The answers to those questions became the "commentary" videos whose contents laid the foundation for the book you're reading. And this experience gave me an idea for what I could do in my post-basketball life, whenever that happened.

Between that time and the spring of 2014, I recorded between 100 and 175 videos a week, and then I decided to take an entire week off. No gym, no drills, and no video recording. Some days I spent writing. Others, I practiced yoga in South Pointe Park. I also read a lot. And finally, I did something that I'd rarely done despite living on 5th Street near Washington Avenue in South Beach: I actually went to the beach.

When I didn't feel completely out of my mind after spending a week away from the gym, I not only knew it was time to leave basketball, I also knew that I could thrive without it.

With that in mind, I started figuring out what was next. I'd already been selling products, including books, training programs for athletes, and online courses, for years. In addition, there were four things I knew for sure:

1. Many members of my original basketball-playing audience had moved on to something other than basketball by the end of their teens. If all I talked about or offered was basketball material, I could no longer serve them.

2. I never wanted to box myself into being just a *basketball guy*. I knew I had a lot to share with people who didn't play or watch sports seriously.

3. I had always been good at breaking down ideas into "bite-sized" portions that anyone could relate to, even if they were unfamiliar with the topic. I did so a lot with basketball, and I could do the same with nonsport concepts that interested me.

4. Ever since I was a kid, I always had a vision of a whole lot of people knowing who I was. With my basketball time done and that goal not quite accomplished, I still needed to be heard.

Now all I needed to do was figure out how to apply those four facts about myself to a new career. I had to take the initiative, because no one was going to just appear out of the proverbial woodwork and provide me with a new way to earn a living. It was up to *me*—just like *your* success is ultimately up to *you*.

FIGURE OUT HOW TO TRANSITION FROM WHAT YOU'RE ALREADY GOOD AT TO SOMETHING NEW

In addition to recording videos, I enjoyed speaking to live audiences. My experiences of class presentations, addressing teammates in basketball, and live streaming online always excited and energized me. But I knew nothing about the business side of it, or if there even *was* a business side to public speaking. My idea for finding out was to do the same thing I'd done in basketball: take massive action, perform as much as I could, even if I had to spend out of pocket to do so, and get people to know my name. *If I'm good at it,* I reasoned, *someone's going to see me, and opportunity will follow.*

I'd been playing in a weekly pickup game, and talking to a guy on the sideline at the end of the games. I told him that I was contemplating the end of my basketball career, and he asked what I planned to do next. I told him that I wanted to become a professional speaker, and he asked me if I'd ever heard of Toastmasters. I told him I had, but I knew nothing about what it was or why anyone would be involved. He explained that it was a place to practice speaking and listening, which sounded like the perfect place for me. I found a local club in Miami Beach and joined at the very next meeting.

I remember attending my first meeting and listening to three people give short, five- to seven-minute speeches. Driving home, I was so excited about giving my own speech that I was already formulating what I'd say and how I'd say it. The day of my "icebreaker," I stood in front of a room of 10 to 15 people and (briefly) told my story.

I told the audience that I had joined to learn how to become a professional speaker. Although I wasn't even sure Toastmasters was the place to learn such a thing (I found out that it's not), I was going to keep taking action until I figured it out.

An ex-NFL All-Pro named Phillip Buchanon was in the room that day. Phil told me he was on the same path, a former athlete going into business. He was attending an event soon where he would meet people who knew the speaking business well. I had a prior commitment and couldn't attend, so Phillip promised me he would connect me with any local people he met that he thought would be of benefit to me.

True to his word, Phillip texted me the name and number of Dawnna St. Louis not too long after our meeting. Dawnna is a well-known, well-traveled speaker with many years of experience in the business world. After reaching out and speaking on the phone, Dawnna suggested we meet the following week and talk about the platform business—"platform" meaning my speaking, writing books, consulting, and generally my path to becoming a thought leader.

We met and talked, and I took a ton of notes. Periodically, Dawnna stopped to ask me if what she was saying was actually helpful. I assured her it was and continued taking notes. Three hours into what was initially supposed to be a 30-minute meeting, I had 10-plus pages of notes. Later that day, I sent Dawnna an e-mail with 30 potential article topics I gleaned from what she had shared with me. She took those ideas and turned those topics into popular LinkedIn articles of her own. Dawnna became a mentor to me, and I learned so much from her.

IF POSSIBLE, OFFER TO WORK FOR FREE TO GAIN EXPERIENCE

Even with all the knowledge from Dawnna, I was still a rookie in this new world. I decided to get my name out there in the simplest way possible and take every possible opportunity to be seen, paid or unpaid. I became involved in Toastmasters, Rotary Club, CreativeMornings, speaking at local detention centers, Skype conferences, and daily YouTube videos and live streams.

A few years later, in the summer of 2017, I was speaking at a conference in Atlanta. The conference did not pay me to appear, and I paid for my own hotel room, travel, and meals. It was an investment in myself, a gamble that I wasn't so sure would pay off. The event organizers had sold me on the "quality" of the attendees who would be in the audience, but I was new and not sure if the organizers were being truthful or just selling me to fill their agenda of presenters. But, like I said, I'd rather do it and regret it than not do it and think back with "what ifs."

It rained the day of my presentation, and I drove to the venue in an unexcited state. As I pulled into the parking garage of the World Congress Center in downtown Atlanta, I thought to myself, *Why did I sign up to speak here?*

But the performer in me woke up at game time. I mentally entered my Zone as soon as I saw the presentation room. Hours ahead of time, I visualized how I would move around the room, where I would deliver certain points, and even where I would meet people for the post-event photographs and videos. I got on stage and did my thing. The audience was engaged, took notes, and actively participated in Q&A.

A few people came up to me afterward to talk about opportunities with their respective organizations. One was from the NCAA, another from the NBA. Another woman asked if I would be interested in working with a major publisher to write a book. The end result is the book you're reading right now.

This is the kind of serendipitous situation that has happened in my life over and over again after I've taken the initiative and taken a risk. They don't *all* happen to work out, but this time, I'm sure glad it did.

• • •

How can you make these types of situations happen for you? Invite this energy into your life by getting active. If you're a presenter, say yes to every chance you get to present. If you're an athlete, play as often and as hard as you can—wherever you can. If you're a writer, write as often as you can!

Luck only happens when preparation meets opportunity.

• • •

How many times had I acted on my own volition and taken action that was not required of me? Had I *not* taken initiative, would any part of the story have happened?

Personal initiative has gotten me jobs, dates, money, and opportunities, none of which would have existed had I idly waited for them to find me.

I've even found opportunities in places that most people would be wise to avoid.

BE A THERMOSTAT AS WELL AS A THERMOMETER

I love online comments sections. I've read and replied to more than 1.5 million comments on my blog, YouTube videos, live streams, and social media posts over the years.

Shortly after I began my one-video-a-day practice on YouTube, more and more developing basketball players began asking me for help. One particular comment gave me the idea for my first product. A commentator suggested that I take the same workouts that I was doing every day, organize them into a program, and make that program available to the public. I replied that I could do that, but such an idea would require time and effort, which meant I would have to charge for the resulting product. If I made it, would people be willing to pay for it? The overwhelming response (in the YouTube video comments) was YES. The first product, HoopHandbook, has processed more than 13,000 orders as of this writing. Even to this day, questions I read in online comments are breeding grounds for future content and products. Even the negative stuff is grist for my mill. As my favorite author Robert Greene says, *everything is material.*

But you have to be careful of what you read in the comments. While I've gotten good ideas from there, comment sections can also be cesspools of human life. One thing I've always stressed to my viewers online is that my aim is for them to graduate from watching to becoming the one being watched. So since this chapter is about acting and taking charge, let's address how to separate the observers from the doers.

There's a lot to look at, read, listen to, and comment on in our world, and the pool of material is only growing wider and deeper by the day. In the following sections, learn how to separate yourself from the watchers and commentators and become the one they comment on.

Thermometers Report the News

Thermometers serve one purpose: to tell the temperature, and that's it. A thermometer observes what's going on and reports it back to you. We are all thermometers at different times and in different ways. When you share an opinion, read, or watch something, you're a thermometer. Something happened, and you saw it. Thermometer experience is responsible for many points shared in this book.

Thermometers do have a use. Sometimes we *want* to know the temperature. I check the weather daily and dress accordingly. When I make a video or write a book, I share it for feedback. If I'm set to make a big move in business, I want my mastermind group to tell me what they know. There are many times when I want a temperature report, so to speak. It helps to have thermometers around.

You want to be careful of how much time you spend in thermometer mode, though. Some people spend their entire lives there, looking at, listening to, and reading about others and telling you about it. Haters and naysayers are thermometers, watching and offering opinions. I don't expect you to want to spend too much time being a thermometer. It's frustrating to be unable to do anything about what you see. Wouldn't it be better to not only *know* what's going on, but also be able to *affect* the situation?

Thermostats Make the News

The thermostat takes the report from the thermometer, decides what to do about it, and immediately does it. If you have a central cooling or heating system at home, your thermostat is working all the time. It gets constant readings from the thermometer and maintains the climate you want.

Thermostats need thermometers to do their job. Making adjustments is hard if we don't know what we're adjusting or what to adjust it to. Good thermostats need good thermometers.

Your coach, mentor, or supervisor is your thermometer, reporting what he or she sees and what he or she thinks about it. You, as thermostat, are empowered to change what the coach sees. Great thermometers help thermostats do their best.

Check Your Temperature

We all are both thermostat and thermometer; the question is, how often and for how long? How much time do you spend watching and commenting compared to being watched and commented on? Many professional teams outside of the United States will employ only one American-born player, if any. Sometimes this is due to league rules; other times it's budget constraints. In many countries and leagues, the role of an American player is not just to be a star performer, but to elevate the games of the "local" players (players who are from the country the team is based in) through his everyday presence. I once asked a professional basketball coach who worked in Spain (a place I never played) how exactly he chooses among so many American players who want to play professional basketball, many of them very good players. The coach replied that his team chose players solely based on the player's ability to solve his team's problems. If his team was young and not good at rebounding, for example, the coach looked for a veteran player who was a strong rebounder and exemplified leadership. If the team's most glaring needs were shooting and ball handling, the coach sought a player who was strong in both. The player who best solved the most problems was the player the coach most wanted.

The same can be true for you at work. Your value in the workspace is based on how many problems are solved by your presence and how efficiently you solve them.

It's good to keep around someone who notices what's going on; even better to have someone who can dictate what goes on.

Thermometers *report* what's happening. Thermostats *are* what's happening.

Next I'll tell you a story of a guy who was a thermostat all by himself, for himself.

——— EXAMINE YOUR GAME ———
What's the mindset you need to be a permanent thermostat?
How can you be the perpetual mood-changer in the room?

THE HUSTLING STARBUCKS EMPLOYEE

I went to Starbucks one day to write. It wasn't long before I noticed an employee who really stood out.

This guy was walking the shop floor, tidying up, refilling stations, and maintaining order. He was hustling in a way that isn't normal for a worker anywhere I've seen. My first instinct upon seeing this guy was that he either:

- Needed to go to the bathroom,
- Was about to get off his shift or go on break, or
- Was new and working to prove himself to the boss.

After sitting in Starbucks for two hours and seeing the hustling employee's interaction with his coworkers and customers, it was clear to me that he was not new. He was not trying to impress: from what I could tell, among the three people working, he *was* the boss. And I never saw him go to the bathroom.

It occurred to me to ask the hustling barista what compelled him to move and work so urgently. But he was working so fluidly that I didn't want to interrupt his flow. I even saw him get on his knees and scrub the floor, which I'd *never* seen anyone do in a Starbucks. He was in a Zone. While working, he also chatted with familiar patrons in English and Spanish, communicated with the two employees working behind the counter, and sang along to every song playing through the shop stereo system.

I was impressed. This guy's manner and hustle reflected an approach that anyone would hire for, regardless of qualifications. With that attitude, skills are secondary and, frankly, a mere formality.

Maybe you've worked with people like this before. They have a positive can-do energy that can make those around them look lazy. Coworkers either admire the hustle, or they are annoyed by how they look like slackers next to them. Either way, no one can question this person's initiative for doing the work.

I didn't speak to the hustling barista, but if I had, I guarantee he'd credit his hustle to something bigger than a blind devotion to Starbucks. Maybe he wanted to set an example for his coworkers. Maybe he wanted his customers to have a great experience. Whatever it is, I'm 99 percent sure it was more than the green apron and hourly wages that were motivating him.

Make a conscious decision to move faster and to get more done, more quickly. People will notice. But although the advice is so simple, few ever use it.

* * *

Every coaching and consulting client I've ever worked with came to me through what I always do: a live stream, video, or being a guest on someone else's show or network. I wasn't out prospecting for a new client; I was doing the best job I could where I was, and opportunity found me. This Starbucks guy, if what I saw from him this day was his normal pace, probably has an opportunity coming his way, if it hasn't already.

Upon first seeing the Starbucks hustler, my first question was not about him, but about myself. Did I move at the pace and with the level of urgency that he had? Although he was doing manual labor and I was writing a book, the question still applied. When either our minds or our bodies have a reason to be urgent, the other party—mind or body—dutifully follows.

It really is that simple. Any thought becomes a habit when you do it often enough.

But why would you even have the thought? What do you stand to gain from, or what reason would you have to be doing, this hustling thing like the Starbucks employee?

EXAMINE YOUR GAME

Can you work harder, better, faster, more efficiently, than you have been? If so, why? And what do you have to do to *continue* doing so even after you've found success?

What if you are just really good at what you do, and you can make it look easy? Maybe you don't need to hustle as hard when you've worked on your game a lot, right? It's not like anyone will notice. Right?

Wrong.

Let me tell you how I learned that I wasn't fooling anyone when, though highly skilled, I still was giving less than my all.

BE SMOOTH, BUT DON'T COAST

After returning home from Lithuania, I spent a few months frequenting the LA Fitness in the Andorra section of Philadelphia. There was a basketball gym there, and I'd been told that's where the best games were taking place. During this time, I was playing the best pickup games I experienced in all my 24 years living in Philadelphia.

On any Monday through Thursday evening, I saw players from the AND1 Mixtape (which was the VHS-tape, grassroots street basketball highlights before the YouTube era), NBA players and their friends, Philly streetball legends, and generally solid, not-famous players who were serious about basketball. You had better be serious to even play in there. The games got so serious that LA Fitness management banned duffle bags and backpacks from the basketball court because people were packing weapons to settle on-court disputes.

One evening, I played several high-intensity pickup games, and one of the guys I had played with stopped me to talk. I had never seen him before that day, and I knew he'd taken a liking to my game. I was 23 at the time, and I would have guessed him to be in his mid- to late thirties. He was the type of guy who commanded respect just by his mere presence. He wasn't threatening or aggressive; he just had a *presence*. And what he said to me really opened my eyes.

"Dre, first of all, you have *game* . . . I saw you do some things today that I've only seen pro guys do. I've played in every league in Philly, and many guys I've played with can't do some of the stuff I saw you do. You *can play*, and I know *you* know that. But I'm gonna tell you something that I'm sure you've been told before. Something I'm sure your coaches have been on you about before. Dre, you coast when you're playing. Half of the time, you're not playing hard."

Never in four years of college did I ever feel I didn't have the *skill* to compete. When I had bumped heads with my coaches, it was always for the same reason: an unwillingness to exert myself past discomfort. This guy, who didn't know me and whom I'd never met, sized me up perfectly and was 100 percent accurate. Damn it!

Playing NCAA Division 3 ball had made this coasting habit even more of an issue. Many of my teammates and opponents didn't have my ability. While I could be a factor without going full throttle, some teammates and opponents had no choice but to play as hard as possible, just to keep up with everyone else. At the same time, I was still a Division 3 athlete: I wasn't *so* talented that I could coast and still win easily. This was the source of my coach's frustrations with me.

Through four years of college, assuming 25 games per season and 40 total minutes for each game, I had played roughly 1,000 of 4,000 possible minutes. Only 200 of those unplayed minutes were due to an injury—knee tendinitis in my sophomore year.

In the LA Fitness Andorra locker room, the man continued his assessment.

"Dre, I have not seen many players who are better than you, talent-wise. You have the tools to do pretty much everything I've seen any other player do. But here's the thing: if you go to one of those leagues, against guys who have the same talent you have, and you *coast*, you won't win. If they're playing hard and you're coasting, they'll beat you every time.

"Here, you're playing against guys who *have* to play as hard as they possibly can just to keep up with you. I'm an older guy, I *have* to play hard to keep up with young guys like you. There were many times in our games where you weren't playing hard at all, Dre. You picked your spots. If you start to play hard all the time, *maybe* you could go somewhere with your game."

I thanked the guy for the talking-to he'd given me, and we parted ways.

The man's words hit me hard. He'd seen me play one time, and play well, and diagnosed the biggest issue of my four years of college. I came to a realization: though I was talented, and

I had developed enough game to be pro-level good, I wasn't fooling anyone by giving less than my best effort. I wrote that phrase down—*be smooth, but don't coast*—and still remind myself of it to this day.

Just because you've gotten good enough to make doing what you do look easy, doesn't mean you should *take it* easy. The more skill you have, the more you'll need to discipline yourself to bring maximum effort—even when you could get by with less.

HAVING GAME IS NOT A FREE PASS TO RELAX

A high skill level is not a free pass to chill out and coast by on ability. Contrarily, it's a mandate to do more.

To whom much is given, much is tested. The more game you have, the more you're depended on to deliver. You are looked at to be the leader in every presentation, in every deal, and in every competition. Your team depends on you to take pressure off of them.

Who runs the anchor leg in a relay race? Usually it's the fastest person who's given the responsibility of closing the deal and winning the race. In a late-game scoring situation in basketball, the ball usually goes to the best player, who decides what to do with it. When there's an important presentation to be made, you call on your best presenters and salespeople.

If you're that best player or anchor-leg runner, understand the responsibility you now have: the team is counting on you to finish the job that they've started. They trust you with this important job because they know what you're capable of—and so do you. Respect the responsibility.

The More Game You Have, the Higher the Expectation to Show It

My time playing in Montenegro wasn't always a picnic. In fact, the gym we played and practiced in, though it was brand new, didn't have a working heating system. I was in the city of Herceg Novi, which is on the Bay of Kotor, and while it doesn't get as cold as, say, Philadelphia in January, it does get cold enough to be uncomfortable.

We practiced with hoodies on. Personally, I hate being cold, even more so when playing basketball. By the time I got to Montenegro, though, I was a veteran of the pro basketball experience and knew what would be expected of me as the only American on the roster: I had to be the best player in the gym every day, even in practice. I pushed myself to show off my athleticism, running and dunking all the time in practices, even in the cold gym and with cold muscles and joints. This did a number on my knees, which were in very bad shape by the following off-season, but I knew I couldn't afford to be less than my best, even in a freezing cold gym. Every time we don't give our best effort, we're not only jeopardizing our positions, but we are weakening ourselves. We are weakened mentally, because unconsciously we know we're doing less than we could, and we are weakened in whichever way—physically, financially, emotionally—we're not working.

And it's not a secret. *Everyone* can see when you're operating at less than full capacity. People know when you're "dogging it," as we say in sports, even when they don't call you on it. Be self-aware enough to call yourself on it.

Hard work is *hard* for a reason. If it were easy, everyone would do it. Your high skill level may tempt you into believing you can "get by" without working hard. And you're actually right: you can get by. But is *getting by* what you want for your life and career?

Maybe you see a bit of yourself in this story. Maybe you want to get to that point, so good that you could afford to scale back your effort. Either way, doing more—not less—with your effort level is the vehicle to your next level of achievement.

THE QUALITY OF QUANTITY

In *The 10X Rule*, Grant Cardone espouses the principle of utilizing energy and activity, doing 10 times the activity you are expected to do to achieve your aims (which should also be 10X'd). How many times have you heard of someone maximizing effort where they lacked skill, connections, or knowledge? The people who embody the literal *rags to riches* stories of our world do it every day, often even after they've achieved success. What's crazy is, many people fail to take action *because* they lack skill and knowledge. Call them out on it, and they'll reiterate how they need to learn more before doing anything.

You probably have heard the saying *quality over quantity*, which suggests that doing it *right*, however you define *right*, is more important than doing it often. In some cases, quality is more important than quantity. Open-heart surgery, marriage, and furniture shopping come to mind as examples. For self-improvement, however, quality is more often an excuse than a real reason to delay action. I know salespeople who won't make a single call before they're sure they have the perfect, proper script. Then, the first call they do make goes completely off-script within five seconds.

Whether you are great or terrible at what you do, experienced or brand-new, you must understand, appreciate, and apply what I call *the quality of quantity* to your life. When you're good at what you do and you know you're good, sometimes it's just an increase in activity that's needed to create the attention and results you feel you deserve.

I've seen and experienced many examples of this: people getting better, or at least being perceived as better, just because they stepped up their activity level. One such story follows.

When You're Really Good, Max out Your Potential!

Working at Foot Locker in 2004, my first job after college, my coworker Rob and I shared an interest in rap music. Rob constantly warned me to get up-to-date and listen to who Rob saw as the hottest rapper in the game at the time: Lil Wayne.

I knew who Lil Wayne was: he'd been around since the nineties rapping both solo and with his group the Hot Boys. I saw Wayne as an OK rapper, but nothing special. What Rob knew that I didn't was that Wayne had begun to flood the streets with his mixtapes, and his fans were eating it up. Lil Wayne had apparently launched a rap-as-much-as-humanly-possible campaign, and between 2005 and 2007, he was probably the most popular rapper on the scene—or as Wayne labeled himself, the "Best Rapper Alive."

Lil Wayne felt he was good enough to hold the crown as the best rapper; a lot of people (like me) were aware of Wayne but saw him as something less than that. Wayne exposed himself and his skill to the world with such quantity that you had the choice of either hating him or loving him for the exact same reason: Lil Wayne was everywhere.

When your game is finally where you want it to be, performance-wise, now it's time to get your game in the right place, location-wise: get active and spread your name (and work) around. Don't allow yourself or your game to be ignored.

When You're *Bad,* You Need as Much Practice as Possible!

What about when you're new, you don't know what you're doing, or you just plain suck at the job? What are you to do? This is the time for you to *Work On Your Game.*

When I sucked at basketball, which was basically all of high school, I used every free moment to go to the local playground and practice by myself. I didn't have a particular strategy for practicing or anyone to follow—this was long before YouTube—but the only way I figured would work to make me better was to practice as much as possible.

It worked.

Kanye West, when trying to break into the music industry as a producer, said he would create five new tracks every day for three consecutive summers. By 2001, Kanye's production was all over Jay-Z's classic *The Blueprint* album.

Practice, play, and perform as much as you possibly can, learning and gaining valuable experience. This is the price of admission—to be good and recognized as such.

Overexposure, Burnout, and "Too Much" Are All Myths

When I explain this quality-of-quantity principle to people, some resist. Many ask me, *What about overexposure or burnout?*

These people fear they'll use up all of their value or run out of ability if they do too much. While I won't invalidate your feelings, tell me how many people you can name whose run ended from doing too much, going too far, making too many sales, dialing too many numbers, or trying too hard to succeed. How many do you know?

I hear of burnout when it refers to CEOs of large companies or super-popular entertainers who tour nonstop. Someone who's hospitalized or forced to rest due to burnout usually reaches this point after *a long period of effort and production*, reaping the benefits of quantity. For every one person you know who did burn out, I can counter with thousands of people and brands who are very active and very much "exposed"—seen and top-of-mind—and doing very well because of it.

People who claim overexposure as a reason for inaction usually have not taken nearly enough action to even approach overexposure. Do you worry about having too much muscle when you've never been to a gym? Do you fear overeating while you're starving? Are you concerned with the problem of too much money when you're broke?

Here's your new mindset: Get there first, handle problems later.

Don't waste time forecasting the possible hardships, because challenges will always be there. And since we're all going to die anyway, would you rather burn out from making maximum use of your resources, or rust out from nonuse, never knowing what could have been?

• • •

As you're doing so much, you need people to know about you and what you're doing. Since they may not always come to you, you need strategies for going to them. I cover that in the next chapter.

8

SELLING YOURSELF

Taking initiative is not only about working harder, making connections, being persistent—all the things I recommended in Chapter 7. Taking initiative also requires that you *reach out* to anyone and everyone you think can help you get to where you want to go. In this chapter, I'll show you how I did that in my career, and I'll give you some suggestions for how *you* can reach out to get where *you* want to go.

BE RELENTLESS ABOUT CONTACTING PEOPLE FOR YOUR NEXT CONTRACT, GIG, OR JOB

In professional basketball, you join a team by signing a contract. When that contract ends—either by the team releasing you for whatever reason or the contract period ending—you're a free agent again, and you have to find a team to play for, again.

By September 2007, I had been under contract three times: in Lithuania, Mexico, and for a traveling show team in the United States. I didn't have a contract in place for my next team, though. I was without an agent, as my first agent was no longer working in basketball, so I opted to employ the best agent I knew: myself.

I decided I would send personalized e-mails to every professional team, everywhere. Any team I could find, I would contact—until I got back on a professional basketball team. I even changed my MySpace profile name to "Not Changing This until I Sign a Contract." Then I went to work.

Over the next four months, I sent thousands of e-mails to hundreds of teams. I got barely as much as a sniff of interest. You may be wondering how I could send *thousands* of e-mails to hundreds of teams. It's simple: I e-mailed the same teams over and over and over again, testing subject lines and content with each iteration. Here are a few of the e-mails I sent:*

From: Dre Baldwin

To: Montenegrin Team Management

Sent: December 4, 2007 5:20:56 AM

Subject: Explosive Scoring Guard—Dre Baldwin

Hello, I would like to join your team! I am in shape and game-ready right now, and I would like to join your team for the

---

* **Note to Basketball Players:** Keep in mind that I used this strategy in 2007; today (more than 10 years later), I do not consider these sample e-mails to be exact templates for you to use to market yourself in a competitive field like pro basketball, as everyone has copied and saturated this technique over the years. If you want to know what I would do if I were starting a career today, google my online article entitled, "10-Step Plan: How I Would Play Basketball Overseas If Starting Today."

remainder of this season, and possibly thereafter if both sides are satisfied. I am bringing scoring, athleticism, rebounding, and excitement to our team. I am willing to come in on a tryout contract if necessary. You will be very satisfied with your decision to add me to you roster. Thanks for your response!

Scouting report: [Link]
Short Video: [Video Links]
Game film upon request.

From: Dre Baldwin
To: [A Lot of Basketball Agents]
Sent: August 18, 2006 8:04 PM
Subject: Dre Baldwin—Seeking Representation

Hello! My name is Dre Baldwin, and I'm currently looking for a contract for the upcoming basketball season. I found your company listed on Eurobasket.com; you seem to be able to find jobs for players pretty well. I have played in Lithuania in 2005; with a traveling-show basketball team (Harlem Ambassadors), and in Mexico. I have included my basketball profile, along with my scouting report from the Infosport Camp I attended. I also have video available if needed. You can reach me at this email address or at my permanent home number, (215) xxx-xxxx. Thanks for your time!

From: Dre Baldwin
To: German Club General Manager
Sent: April 20, 2008 2:47 PM
Subject: Dre Baldwin

Markus, how are you, and how did the season go? I have a game film that I want to send to you, so give me your address to get the DVD. When do you begin practicing for next season so you can bring me over? Thanks!!

In early December, a team in Montenegro replied to me. They liked my game (I had shared some game footage in my e-mail), and they were interested in signing me for the rest of the season. They wanted to vet me, though, and make sure I was who I said I was before offering me a deal.

It just so happened that this Montenegrin team's general manager had a few American friends. These American friends were a married couple who lived 25 minutes from me in Florida. This couple just so happened to spend time in Montenegro every summer, which is how they knew the team personnel. The team arranged for me and the American couple to meet.

A week later, I was signed and moved into my apartment in Herceg Novi, Montenegro.

You can see from the e-mail–sending part that I was willing to hustle to make something happen. But then you have this American couple, who *just so happened* to spend time in Montenegro, and *just so happened* to know the team GM, and *just so happened* to live in the *one* part of the United States in which I also lived?

Luck? Happenstance? Maybe. But what is luck? Luck is when *preparation meets opportunity*. My hours on the courts had *prepared* me, and I created the *opportunity*. *Then* I got lucky.

Another definition for luck is the energy of initiative creating favorable circumstances. You've probably had things like this happen to you before, and because you believe in it, they'll happen again.

Montenegro was the first pro opportunity I created 100 percent by myself, with no agent and no personal connections. Although I already believed it theoretically, Montenegro proved that I could create a fire by rubbing two sticks—amateur-edited video and unyielding persistence—together. Getting back in the pros in 2007 was an outbound job. I couldn't afford to wait for the phone to ring or my inbox to light up. I had decided to make as many waves as possible, *until* something happened.

Here's how to use the outbound mindset to make an opportunity to get lucky.

Reach out to One Person per Day Who Could Further Your Cause

I met Tamara in Croatia in 2011. A Serbian, Tamara had played college basketball in the United States. Knowing that many foreign-born players long to come to the United States to play NCAA basketball, I asked Tamara how she had managed to make it happen.

"I mailed footage of myself to every college coach on the East Coast of the U.S.," she said. Tamara kept up the practice until she connected with a coach who was interested and had the resources—like an open roster spot—to take her in. Tamara went on to have a successful professional basketball career as a player and a coach.

To play the outreach strategy, first know your goals: decide what you want to have, what you need to do, and who you need to be. Then, reach out to at least one person per day who could help you become it, do it, or have it. The good thing for you now (as opposed to me back then) is that there are myriad ways to reach people. Anyone who is not purposely hiding can easily be found online. Utilize face-to-face encounters, phone calls, tweets, comments, direct messages, e-mails, InMail, private snaps on Snapchat, and anything else at your disposal to make contact.

What do you say when you make contact? Be honest! Get to the point with the important stuff: who you are, what you're doing, what you want. If you're offering something in exchange—which always helps—include that. Be brief and cut out all nonessential info. If people want to know more, they'll ask for more.

Promote Your Sh*t!

Whatever you choose to do, you'll need the cooperation of other people at some point. You'll need staff to work for you, partners to invest in you, customers to buy from you, an audience to listen to you. When you connect with these people, make your work visible!

Some people get antsy about self-promoting. They don't like getting in people's faces (figuratively speaking). They don't want to feel like they're being "salesy." Many people would rather all the opportunities *come to them* rather than going out to the opportunities.

Hell, me too! But luck doesn't happen that way.

When I started sending those e-mails, I wanted every team in the world to respond in either one of two ways:

1. Reply and talk to me, or
2. Mark all messages from address Dre@DreAllDay.com as spam

Indifference was the one thing I wouldn't accept.

If you don't like promoting, selling, and drawing attention to yourself, you should develop a dislike for eating, feeding your family, and living the life you want to live. All of life is a sale. If you have this problem, you've just sold yourself on not being a salesperson—and did so successfully! Which means you *can* sell—you just need a new product.

Say YES to Everything Until Your Phone Is Ringing off the Hook

Many people approach life with a "No" attitude, protecting what they have and viewing anything new and unfamiliar with wary eyes. These people operate as if the goal is to stay exactly where they are and never advance. They wake up one day wondering why life is so boring and they've stagnated for the last 17 years.

Look at your current life. If you want more, want to become more, or wish to do more, your reach must expand. Start with your thinking.

────────── EXAMINE YOUR GAME ──────────

Be open to new experiences, and say YES to
everything until you're so busy and your calendar
so full that you have to start saying no!

If you're an athlete, say yes to every offseason game and league until you have a game every day of the week. If you're a speaker or want to be one, say yes to every stage opportunity until your calendar is full.

If you're an author, blogger, or journalist, write every day until you can sell your products or be paid to write.

The person with initiative says yes—even when not quite sure how he'll get it done.

If you're saying yes so often, you'd better be good at what you do and utilizing the opportunities to get better.

But some people don't know exactly how to get better. I have that covered, too.

HOW TO GET BETTER AT ANYTHING, AT ANY TIME

Ask anyone if they want to get better at what they do, whether it be a job or hobby or a side passion, most people will say yes. But many people don't know how exactly to get better. People reach plateaus in their growth and either become too complacent with where they are, stall out for lack of information, or just stop trying to improve altogether.

The steps that follow are what you need to follow in order to continuously grow—even when you feel stuck.

Step 1: Know Where You Really Are

If you call Delta airlines to book the next flight to Seattle, the agent's first question will be where you're flying from. If you tell the agent that you're in Dallas when you're actually in Chicago, you'll never make it to Seattle (not on Delta's DFW-SEA flight, at least). You can't go where you want to go if you're unclear about where you're starting from.

I notice this affliction often in dealing with athletes. Athletes are conditioned to be confident and have a high level of belief in their skills. That's one reason why many athletes have a hard time honestly assessing themselves, along with the lack of perspective any of us has in assessing ourselves without outside input. A player gets cut from his varsity basketball team, but claims he was "by far" the best player in the gym.

Confidence is about having full belief and conviction in what you can do; it's also being honest enough with yourself to know what you lack. Trust yourself enough to be honest about where you are.

Step 2: Ask Yourself, What's the Ideal?

Now that you know where you are, get a clear read on how far you need to go. When setting goals for myself, I assess every area of my life. I mentally take myself through each day of the past week and visualize what every area of my life would look like at its best. I include as much detail as I can. I also ask the following questions:

- *What do I want?*
- *Where do I want to be?*
- *Who do I want to be?*
- *How do I want it to happen?*
- *How much money do I want, exactly?*
- *How many points do I want to score each game?*
- *What position do I want to be promoted to?*
- *How much revenue do I want my business to do?*
- *What type of boyfriend or girlfriend or car or house or kids or family do I want to have?*

──── EXAMINE YOUR GAME ────

Go into dream mode and write out what
your ideal outcome looks, feels, and sounds
like. Don't leave out any details.

Step 3: Identify the Most Important Step You Can Take Right Now

When I finished college with plans to play professional basketball, my first planned step was to sign with an agent. An agent could do many things I didn't know how to do including contact professional teams, get a team interested in me, negotiate a contract, and get my next job lined up while I was still in the current one.

The only problem was, agents weren't interested in representing me. So I set out to answer the big question why. The answer seemed to revolve around the fact that I was unproven at the pro level. But I still wanted an agent, so my revised first step was to gather the collateral that would make an agent care. I needed proof that I could excel while playing against pros. After attending that first exposure camp, I had said collateral, and I signed with my first agent shortly thereafter.

Life's possibilities are endless. Think of all the things you could be doing right now instead of reading, for exmaple. All the places you could be instead of being where you are. All the different jobs you could have instead of the one you do have. With so many possibilities on our minds, we grow less and less focused as our attention spans shorten.

Counteract possibility overflow by asking yourself these really good questions:

- *What's the most important step I can take right now?*
- *Who's the first person I can call?*
- *What is the first chapter of my book?*
- *What's the first product I can create?*
- *Which gym can I get a membership to?*

Answer each question, then do it. Follow these steps every time you want to get better, and you will never fail to improve.

PLAN A VS. EVERYTHING ELSE

Sean "Puff Daddy" Combs started Bad Boy Entertainment in 1993, and the record label shot quickly to the top. Puffy, as we called him, oversaw projects from several artists in his stable, most notably the Notorious B.I.G., whose debut *Ready to Die* album stamped himself and Bad Boy as the hottest rapper and label in hip-hop.

Tragedy struck when B.I.G. was shot dead in 1997, leaving the hip-hop industry, and Bad Boy especially, in shock. Minus their headline artist, it seemed as if the glory days of Bad Boy were over.

Puffy had been involved in the music business for some time by this point, but he had never picked up a microphone to be the artist himself. In the wake of B.I.G.'s passing, Puffy had two choices:

- Option 1 was to shut down Bad Boy and get out of the music game.
- Option 2 was to push all his remaining chips into the middle of the table, bet on himself, and give himself no way out.

Puffy chose Option 2, literally: his *No Way Out* album, released in July of 1997, was the #1 album on the Billboard charts, sold more than 7 million copies, and marked the beginning of an era in hip-hop where Puffy & co. dominated not only rap, but all of pop music.

Plan Bs are for losers. Literally. Think about it: When is Plan B enacted? When you lose out or give up on Plan A. So how about we make Plan A a foolproof strategy?

Your Plan B exists only when you don't believe strongly enough in Plan A. When you're all-in on Plan A, you do whatever it takes to make Plan A work, including using the resources you would have applied to Plan B.

There are three requirements:

1. Your Plan A is largely based on you and your actions alone.
2. You have to care enough about Plan A to push through the pain, tough days, and walk-away moments (the setbacks that would make most people walk away from the plan) that most people succumb to.
3. You are willing to discard, ignore, and separate yourself from anyone who insists on having a Plan B just in case Plan A doesn't work out. There is no "just in case"; Plan A is the only case.

This *sounds* good, but you never know what might happen. Things may not go the way you planned. And I'll tell you right now: things will *not* work out the way you planned. But this has nothing to do with your decision to reach your destination.

Would it hurt you to have a Plan B, C, or D, though? Yes. It would hurt you. The very act, mentally or physically, of making a Plan B, C, or D is a message to your subconscious mind that you are not 100 percent sure Plan A will work. And it becomes a self-fulfilling prophecy.

But hey, maybe it's the truth: You *aren't* quite sure of Plan A. If so, reread the chapters on Confidence and Mental Toughness.

But if you insist, I'll give you plans B through F, as they should be.

Plan B: New Ideas

Come up with 10 new ideas for making Plan A work. What have you not tried yet? *Hint:* If you have not yet reached your goal, there is *something* you have not yet tried. Ask yourself the question over and over and over again until you have actionable answers.

Before embarking on the e-mailing bonanza that landed me in Herceg Novi, Montenegro, I'd had several other ideas:

- Fly to a country and ask multiple teams for a week-long tryout
- Attend more exposure camps
- Contact agents instead of the teams themselves

If the team-contacting idea hadn't worked, one of the above would have—or I would have died trying.

Plan C: Who Do I Need to Be?

What you're doing is not as important as *who you're being* while you do it. What type of person do you need to become to make Plan A work?

Here's a follow-up question: are you *being* that person right now?

When I first started speaking professionally—or more accurately, *trying* to, I thought it would be a good idea to ignore my sports background. I was talking to businesspeople, after all, not athletes. What businessperson wanted to hear about my life in basketball? How could that possibly relate to their challenges? It turned out the answer was more than I realized. Once I started leveraging the fact that I was an athlete and I could explain how it translated to the business world, things started working for me.

Plan D: Who Can Help Me?

Relationships are a great resource. Tap into the people you know and people you don't know. Ask yourself:

- *Who has been where I want to go?*
- *Who's there right now?*
- *Who can help me get to the next step?*
- *Who can look at my situation and tell me exactly what to do next?*
- *Who is a whole lot smarter than I am and can see things that I would never notice?*

Plan E: Check Yourself

- *Have I put enough energy into this yet?* Answer honestly.
- *Have I been completely dedicated consistently?*
- *Have I been in high-activity mode long enough to even expect results yet?*

These questions, especially the last one, led to my 2007 e-mail blitz, my video-a-day YouTube habit, and the hustle that got me on many stages as a speaker.

Does your activity level match the outcomes that you want? If you put a higher level of energy into anything (even the wrong thing), you'll get some form of results. If you're getting no results whatsoever in either direction, your energy needs a boost.

Plan F: Forget Everyone Who Isn't on Board with You

One challenge with a solo Plan A is the people around you. Some will tell you how dangerous or unwise it is to have only one plan. This is not the time to grow tentative—this is when you double down on your commitment. Anyone who is telling you to give up is a person who's given up. Don't take advice from people who quit on their own goals; that's all they know and thus all they can tell you. Avoid people who've quit on their own Plan A, yet want to tell you yours won't work.

As much as you'd protect your smartphone, wallet, or home, protect your mind from anyone who says your Plan A won't work. If you're the forgiving type, you can come back for them and share a laugh about it later after you've proven them wrong.

• • •

Selling yourself is a job. If you want people to know who you are, you have to be where they are, showing your game. Commit to continually improving and exhaust every option before you give up trying for something that matters to you, because there will be countless people fighting hard to take your spot.

9

———————•———————

YOUR INTERPERSONAL GAME

Working on your mental game is the best thing you can do for your self-development. But eventually, you have to leave your house and interact with people. People you're tasked with leading or following. People you want to sell your goods to. People you want to have a favorable impression of you. Negative people who haven't yet read this book. Lazy, unproductive people you wish to motivate. People dependent on you to help them. Losers who don't want to win and who don't understand why winning is so important to you.

In this chapter, you'll learn how to apply the Work On Your Game mindset—which you've developed from reading this far—to help you deal with others.

MANAGING POLITICS IN YOUR CAREER LEADS TO BETTER RELATIONSHIPS

You may work in a highly political environment, where everyone is angling for power, trying to get close to the right people and staying away from the dangerous people. You work hard to make yourself look good while still watching your back for any friend who could turn foe if it would help him or her get ahead. Not to mention the times when politics has seemingly hurt you. Maybe you've been passed over for a promotion, or blamed for something you had nothing to do with, or gotten negative energy from someone you did nothing to provoke.

The whole environment can be stressful and tiring.

In this context, *politics* means promoting and protecting your own interests. We tend to blame "politics" when subjective human opinion (which we all have) rules against us. When that same subjective opinion decides in our favor, we call it "networking" or "having connections." They're two sides of the same coin—a coin called relationships. Knowing the right people and having key relationships is not luck, it's a skill.

As the saying goes, as soon as you place three people in a room, you'll have politics. Politics is a part of the human existence. It's about time you learn to make politics work for you instead of against you.

If politics is working against you, it's your fault. Take a hard look at yourself and ask these questions:

- *Why don't I have more friends?*
- *Why have I not made more allies?*
- *Why have I not made peace with my enemies?*

It's your job to have the right people in the right places who know, like, and trust you. This is a requirement if you yearn for influence in any profession, group, or organization. When you need a Realtor or a lawyer, what do you do first: do you search online, or do you ask your friends, family, and neighbors who they know? You would probably prefer the referral, because there's some level of built-in trust there. And guess what? Other people think the same way.

Maybe you're not the gregarious, friend-making type. You don't like networking and building relationships; you'd rather just do your work, and do it so well that relationships don't matter. Well, someone has to buy your work, and people can't do that if they don't know you. Get a friend, business partner, manager, or agent who loves getting to know people.

———————————— EXAMINE YOUR GAME ————————————

Step out of your comfort zone and make friends. Or get used to being overqualified and overskilled for the position you're in.

There are websites and apps whose sole purpose is to help you meet new people (and they're *not* all dating-based). Learn how to start and maintain a conversation, keeping the talk centered on what the other person wants to talk about. We all like to talk about ourselves, and we come to like people who allow us to do so.

If people don't trust you or know what to expect from you, you're at fault. Trust builds from discipline. Your disciplined performance—*consistent with very little variation over time*—helps people trust you. Think of a traffic light, for example. We know its pattern and exactly how it works. And when traffic lights malfunction, there's total chaos. What we trust and can predict, we depend on and value. Be this for others.

Utilize what you learned in Chapter 2 and become more consistent in your work performance. Identify what you can offer, and be consistent with it. I told you how I started my brand: people liked seeing my basketball drills every day, so I published new drills every day. People came to trust me and my delivery, which built a reputation.

IMPROVE YOUR PEOPLE SKILLS

I want to address two key people skills: conversation and caring.

To be a good conversationalist, you need two tools. One is an ability to ask questions. Not just any questions, but open-ended questions that get or allow others to talk. The other is your ability to carry on a conversation. The easiest way to do this is by actively listening while others talk, not thinking of what you'll say next. Listening is hearing not just what's said, but also what's not said, noticing the energy behind people's words, and empathizing to feel what they are feeling. Empathy is the sharing of feelings.

Remember that most communication is nonverbal. Pay close attention to everything around people's words. Nonverbal cues communicate feeling. Try making yourself feel what another person is feeling and you build rapport, which unconsciously builds trust.

Develop a base of allies. Friends are not only for social media popularity. Friends can do things for you that you could not do yourself. And even if you could do them, there is only one you. You can be in only one physical location at a time. You can focus on only one thing at a time. Having allies doing things on your behalf saves you time, energy, money, and any other resource. Allies also *create* those resources.

Now, this is not about *using* people: the more capable you are of doing things to help others, the more valuable you become to them, as well. Leverage your own skills to forge strategic alliances with those who are where you want to be. If there's a specific hard-to-get-to person you want to meet, make friends with that person's associates and see what happens. This isn't a foolproof strategy guaranteed to work, but it's better than doing nothing. Continue developing your game, while making connections with people who are doing the same.

EXAMINE YOUR GAME

How often are you making new connections?
And how much are you staying in touch
with your established connections?

But no matter how nice and friendly you are, there are bound to be some negative people out there. People who will always find a way to talk down on you for no good reason. How do you deal with negativity and constructive or destructive criticism?

OVERCOME SELF-CRITICISM AND LEARN HOW TO DEAL WITH CRITICISM FROM OTHERS

I meet a lot of entrepreneurs who don't want to sell their goods. That's a crazy concept, since selling stuff is the very essence of entrepreneurship. But it's the truth: many entrepreneurs are terrible, reluctant salespeople. You can imagine what kind of effect this has on their businesses. The following are the objections I hear most often.

- "I need more knowledge before I try selling anything."
- "I don't want to be all 'sales-y,' pushing my products and services on people."
- "I'd rather have people come to me; I don't want to go to them."
- "I don't have the qualifications (college degree, certifications, some other random documentation) to put myself out there any further."
- "I don't know if anyone will be interested."
- "I don't want to bother people while they're at work/at home/enjoying their time off/alive and breathing."

James Altucher, author of *Choose Yourself*, offers a great idea for parsing people's explanations. James says every explanation offers a *good* reason, with a *real* reason behind it.

To some, any of the above is a reasonably good reason. None of the above excuses, though, is the real reason. Maybe you *are* ignorant of a subject, and you *don't* want to be a pushy salesperson, and your resume is *not* impressive. There are plenty of people with the same limitations who were not stopped from doing what they wanted to do anyway.

The real reason for the above list is a fear of being judged. But it goes deeper than that. You're not so much afraid of judgment from other people; you are really afraid of judgment from yourself.

Jack Canfield, author of the *Chicken Soup for the Soul* series, analogizes external criticism to Velcro. A person's criticism can stick to you only when there's already something in your mind— that other piece of Velcro—that believes it at some level.

A fellow basketball player once told me my shooting technique "looked funny" and offered some suggestions for what I should change. What my shot *looked like* wasn't important to me; what mattered was if the ball was going in the basket or not, and how often. Let's say, on the other hand, someone told me to comb my messy hair. I wouldn't be bothered in the slightest. Look at my photo at the end of this book to see why.

Criticism bothers us only if we agree with it at some level. For the sales-challenged entrepreneurs, the imagined criticism is not about other people. It's what the entrepreneur already feels about himself. The supposed judgments of others are the scapegoats that protect them from admitting to being afraid of themselves, which sounds kind of silly.

I hear people self-criticize—in a bad way—often. This is not the healthy, make-myself-better form of critique. Some call it "being my own biggest critic." What you're really seeing is their everyday self-talk happening out loud. Some examples:

- "How bad I look in a picture."
- "How dumb I sound on video or audio."
- "How pointless my writing is."
- "How no one would ever buy my stuff; my current lack of buyers serving as proof."
- "How I always _____ [bad habit], which is reinforced every time I speak."
- "_____ [Insert your top self-criticism here]."

Have you ever considered hypnotizing yourself? Your self-talk is hypnotizing you with every thought. Taking control of this self-hypnosis is the goal of my book *The Mental Handbook*.

Maybe you would defend the behaviors above in the name of holding yourself accountable. This is how you communicate to make yourself better, you say. Look, there's nothing wrong with identifying areas for improvement. There's nothing wrong with being unsatisfied with where you are and what you've done to this point. Striving for perfection is a good thing, if that's what you're truly after. But the self-criticism I'm describing here hurts your results more than it helps. This form of self-critique dents your confidence, slows your production, and kills initiative, all resulting in lower levels of achievement.

Perhaps you self-criticize, truly intending to push yourself to be your best. I say, to hell with intentions. What is the outcome your intentions achieve? Imagine a stranger punched you in the face and gave you a black eye. Would it acceptable if he explained that his benign intention was to swat an insect off your head?

What matters more, intentions or outcomes?

Everything you do produces an outcome, even if that outcome is stagnation. The *outcomes* of your actions, words, and thoughts—not the intentions—are what matters. Criticism destroys potential every day. The fatal brand of criticism is not from a coach, supervisor, or hater. They cannot affect you without your consent. Your own never-ending self-criticism is killing you the most.

In *Think and Grow Rich*, Napoleon Hill placed the fear of poverty at the top of his list of human fears. Given the state of the economy when he wrote his book, which was during the Depression, this made sense. The next fear on Hill's list is the fear of criticism. More people stop themselves over fear of what they *think* others would think or say about them. It's really what you say to yourself that's holding you back.

GIVE YOURSELF PERMISSION TO BE UNPERFECT

Few people enjoy failing, coming up short, or missing a target. So, we self-criticize to preempt any failure-possible action.

Think of your most significant achievements. You probably didn't get everything right on the first try. You may be less than perfect even now. But you still get it done. How? By mentally freeing yourself from an unrealistic need to be perfect, and dealing with the inevitable miscues.

Many publicly successful businesspeople failed numerous times before their big breaks. Michael Jordan had a TV commercial detailing the many times he missed possible game-winning shots for his team.

No human being is perfect. You know that. Criticizing yourself for being less than perfect is a losing habit, because you'll always be less than perfect. Yes, Work On Your Game, give your best effort, and play to win. Understand that things won't always bounce your way, and that's a part of the game.

But you need to stay in the game, despite your imperfections. The worst phrase any human could ever say is, "I could have."

There's the regret of never doing what you could have done, versus the experience of trying, learning, then going back at it. To bring your best effort to your next try, you need your best self available. Stop beating yourself up with undue criticism. Allow yourself to be unperfect, less than *the* best, while learning and still giving *your* best.

When we criticize ourselves, we're usually not plainly stating only the facts. We make it worse by taking each shortcoming to its furthest extent. Someone messes up and says, *I'm always doing this*. Many a basketball player comes to me with the same problem: he had a bad game, missed several shots in a row, and now feels he's a bad shooter who needs to reconstruct his entire skill set. (It doesn't help that we live in an era of everyone wanting to make themselves look better than they are thanks to social media.) If it's so easy to take things to the negative, do the same with the positive! Get and keep reminders around you that reinforce positive up-talk. These can be photographs, trophies, thank you letters, or mementos from happy moments. The positive talk and reinforcing elements, if you use them, will manifest change in your day-to-day life.

USE YOURSELF AS THE STANDARD: COMPETE AGAINST *YOURSELF*

Compete with your personal potential, not with a "should" you made up out of thin air (as discussed in the section on excuses in Chapter 4). Your only competition is the you from yesterday. It's a true cliché. But let's edit this the WOYG way: your only competition is you *at your full potential*.

When you compete against "should," you can't win. No matter what you achieve, there's always another elusive "should" for you to chase. "Should" presumes that you're somehow behind schedule, not where you're expected to be by now—a perfect concoction for self-criticism.

Instead of "shoulds" perpetually playing the carrot and the stick game with you, ask yourself the following:

- *What am I capable of that I haven't yet done?*
- *What's the next immediate step I can take in closing this gap?*

Those questions are your competition.

MANAGE EXTERNAL CRITICISM BY UNDERSTANDING THE CRITICS ARE TALKING TO *THEMSELVES*

When people criticize you, they're taking their internal feelings and projecting them onto you. Looking in the mirror is uncomfortable for some people. When they don't like what they see, that energy has to go somewhere—so as long as there are people, there will be criticism. We are as acutely perceptive of others' flaws as we are blind to our own. Plus, if I can notice something wrong with you, instead of with myself, I'm not responsible for the problem, the work, or the results.

What about when people don't necessarily criticize you, but try to get in your way? What if you feel you're being hated on, discriminated against, or are not one of the "favorites" who get all the breaks? What's the best strategy for dealing with this?

Remember: A True Hit Cannot Be Stopped

In the late aughts, a rapper publicly complained that disc jockey DJ Khaled wasn't playing said rapper's music enough. The rapper claimed that Khaled was playing political games, aiming to appease Khaled's industry friends rather than playing the best available music. Khaled's response is an example of the over-the-top mentality I described in Chapter 2:

> *If you want your music played, make better music. A hit record can't be stopped. No executive, DJ, or politics can stop a hit record.*

Khaled explained that the public demands great music, and if an artist makes great music, people will find it. A hit record, great worker, star entrepreneur, or top athlete is going to shine. Others can stay in the way for only so long before the truth is obvious. Keep this in mind when dealing with haters, politics, discouragers, and self-targeted negativity.

When you truly have the juice, it will happen. From the time I graduated college in 2004 through the summer of 2005, all I wanted was a chance to play professional basketball. I didn't know how to do it, but the desire was there. Anyone who asked me about my future heard about my basketball plans. My only resources were my belief and an expectation that something, anything, would happen soon.

Things did happen. I started writing about my experiences and sharing them online. I soon learned there were a lot of players in the situation I had been in. They were looking for a way into the game but didn't know where to begin. I became their resource.

Get better at what you do by utilizing whatever you have. Stay active and accumulate experience. Learn, experiment, and analyze. Then share value until you become the person, place, or thing people go to or look for in that space. Then, you become the person giving opportunities, not just looking for them.

When You Have a Hit, the Public Chooses You

In 2010, Kevin Systrom launched an app called Burbn.* After Burbn had been out for some time, Kevin knew it wasn't close to being a game-changing entity. He and a business partner went to work to improve the app. They decided Burbn had too many features, and they decided they should focus on Burbn being

---

* "How Instagram Grew from Foursquare Knock-Off to $1 Billion Photo Empire," Eric Moskowitz, *Inc.* magazine, https://www.inc.com/eric-markowitz/life-and-times-of-instagram-the-complete-original-story.html.

great at one specific thing to better grab the public's attention. Noticing that Burbn's photo-sharing capability was its most popular feature, the creators stripped the app down to leave only three features: photos, commenting, and likes. They combined the words "instant" and "telegram," renaming it Instagram.

Launching Instagram on October 6, 2010, the founders knew an app would take some time to populate App Stores worldwide, and looked forward to finally getting a good night's sleep after weeks of long work hours. Within only a few hours, however, Instagram had 10,000 users; 100,000 by the end of the first week. Then 100,000 more the next week. There were more than one million Instagram accounts by mid-December 2010. The app didn't have a big ad campaign or some celebrity endorser. The public deemed Instagram a certified hit.

If you are as good as you say you are and deliver on your promise, nothing can get in your way—not negative people, not past situations, not politics, nothing. The people will demand you—and they'll get you, one way or another.

EXAMINE YOUR GAME

When you find yourself stuck, not catching on,
so to speak, take a hard look at your offering
and see what changes are needed.

Look at your product, service, work style, communication, and yourself as a person. Either something is in the way, or something is missing.

The old saying was, "The cream always rises to the top." The new saying is, "The hit record always gets played."

And when you do make those hit records, attention follows. Just as food attracts ants, attention draws scrutiny. What do you do if you're being unjustly attacked?

"Respek on My Name"

Rapper/entrepreneur Brian "Baby" Williams, also known as Birdman, is CEO of legendary music label Cash Money Records. Birdman made a brief but memorable appearance at The Breakfast Club radio show in 2016. The two-minute conversation became an instant viral hit.*

Before the interview even began, Birdman let the three hosts know that their past comments about him and his company were not appreciated and would not be tolerated. The phrase many people remembered from Birdman's short appearance was, "Put some respect on my fuckin' name." In Birdman's thick southern accent, "respect" sounded like "respek."

Many jokes and memes came out of the situation, most notably Birdman's perceived sensitivity and his pronunciation of the word *respect*. But I saw something different. I saw a person willing to defend the honor of his name, and his willingness to make it publicly known.

Regardless of what you think of the incident or if you even know who these people are, Birdman's stance is pivotal to the Mental Game. You must have the utmost respect for your own game, your work, and the conversation around both. Be willing to defend it when and how necessary. Maybe you think it silly for grown people to be angry about what other people say about them. Sticks and stones break bones, but words can never hurt, right?

---

* https://www.youtube.com/watch?v=4jLT7GQYNhI.

You're right: words *are* just words. But words are also more than just words. If you're a fan of yourself, you must draw a line. The line is the respect you have for your name and anything associated with your name.

Here's how to put and keep Respek on your name.

Never Allow People to Talk Crap About You If They Have Accomplished Less Than You

Rapper Jay-Z was a part-owner of the Brooklyn Nets NBA franchise for several years. Jay would speak of his ownership stake in his songs. Some curious media went looking to find out just how much of the Nets Jay-Z actually owned.

Reports spread of Jay-Z owning no more than 1 percent total of the team. Some reports said it was as little as one-fifteenth of 1 percent. This information would be shared in a mocking sort of way, as if to ridicule Jay-Z's minority ownership. The Brooklyn Nets, according to *Forbes* at the time of this writing, are worth $1.8 billion. 1 percent of that is $18 million. One-fifteenth of 1 percent is $1.2 million. Jay-Z rapped in songs how his alleged 1 percent stake in the Nets, if true, was still more than most people had ever seen in their lives, yet they talked about it as if it were an everyday thing.

Though it can hurt us to do so, we like to compare. We want to see how we're doing measured against what others are doing, or at least *what we think* they're doing. When people see *you* doing and achieving more than they are, they're faced with a conundrum. On one hand, the comparison can be a motivator to drive them to higher heights. This is the less-taken road, though. Why? Because it takes time and effort. Many people are unconsciously unwilling to make that investment, though they *say* they want to get better.

There's another option people have when they see you ahead of them. They can create a story that pulls you down, at least in their minds, that closes the gap between you and them. *You got lucky, you didn't really earn your spot.* The story doesn't need to be true. Holding this story in their minds, a person can sleep at night knowing that you're in front of him only because you had some advantage not available to him. In that person's mind, the gap between you and him or her is now closed.

The more you achieve, the more this happens. Only some of it will you know about.

Though this is mostly a mental game people play with themselves, some will come out and say it. Some critics of Jay-Z's ownership spoke publicly. You don't need to play Birdman and reply to any negatives thrown at you if you don't want to. But have your mental armor ready: understand who it comes from and *why* they do it. It's not about you, it's their way of dealing with themselves.

YOUR WORK AND YOUR NAME ARE CONNECTED

When people refer to their job or business, I've sometimes heard, "It's what I do, but it's not who I am." This is a garbage mindset that should be immediately expunged. Someone created this saying to mentally separate themselves from the work they produce, which is impossible. I'll explain why.

For most of us, our lives are divided into thirds: One-third sleep, one-third work, one-third everything else (fun, family, extra work, etc.). Half the time we're awake, we're doing some form of work. Even if your job or business is not your true passion, the effort you put into it is a reflection of your character.

When someone describes you, what you do for a living is usually part of the description. Whether you want them to or not, people will identify you by what you do.

I'm not telling you that you must tether your human existence to your job. What I'm telling you is that your existence is *already* tethered to your job by everyone who knows what you do. I know there is a whole lot more to you as a person besides only your work. However, we judge people by what they do and what we can see; you can use yourself as a test case. You spend a lot of time working. This makes your work a part of you.

When your work is being disrespected, make an example of one dissenter and the rest will quiet down. The saying goes, "Strike the shepherd and the sheep will scatter." When people trash-talk you, they're not after you. They're after the people who are listening. The trash-talker wants to make an impact on you, on the crowd, or both. Notice when any negative opinions around your name are getting out of control, and address them at their source.

Have you ever watched a *National Geographic* show where the cameras track a pride of lions? If so, you've seen the inevitable confrontation that transpires after a lion has made a kill. A pack of hyenas come to take the carcass away. I saw one scene where a lone lion killed one of the approaching hyenas just to send a message to the rest of the pack. That lion kept its dinner that night.

You don't need to be confrontational with everyone or go around looking for conflict. You do, however, need to be willing and able to defend your name as necessary.

——————————— EXAMINE YOUR GAME ———————————

Your name is the only thing you really own. Treat your name with respect, and others will follow suit.

LET OTHERS FALL IF THEY CHOOSE TO; DON'T FALL WITH THEM

Maybe you really like helping people, almost to a fault. Maybe you're the most successful person in or from your environment, and many people want your help. Maybe you care a lot for a few special someones. But somehow, you've found yourself helping more than you expected to be helping. And now you feel obligated to see it through. What's more, the people you're helping aren't doing much to help themselves.

Sometimes athletes come to me asking for help, guidance, or assistance on things they frankly should be doing for themselves. I tell them as much. This section is for the mothers, fathers, teachers, spouses, significant others, and friends who find themselves giving more effort to another person's success than that person is giving to his or her own success.

Here's how to help them *and* yourself for the long run.

Here's the bottom line: people unwilling to help themselves don't deserve your time and effort.

For example, I get e-mails from mothers and girlfriends who want to help their college-aged sons and boyfriends make it in basketball. The situations always sound the same. A young man is very skilled at the game. He has either made some mistakes in his past or just hasn't been granted the right opportunities. He may be on his last attempt at making it in basketball. Loving mom or girlfriend wants to help him succeed. She does some research and finds Dre Baldwin. Mom asks me for information she can relay to the basketball player for him to do what he needs to do. My response to these messages goes something like this:

I appreciate your message, and I respect the fact that you are willing to help your son/boyfriend make it in basketball.

However, at his age, this is not your battle to fight.

If he is serious about playing basketball, he should be the one e-mailing me, not you. As much as you want to help, you can't want it for him more than he wants it for himself. The fact that you, and not your son/boyfriend, are e-mailing me tells me that you're doing too much.

At this point in his basketball career, he needs to take full control over his destiny and actions. If he's not willing to do so, you need to let him fail, as hard as that may be for you. Basketball is his chosen career, not yours. If he's serious about it, he will take the necessary actions. If he's not serious, he won't make it anyway, regardless of what you do.

I hope you understand where I'm coming from. Feel free to forward this message to your son/boyfriend and have him reach out to me if he so chooses.

Your number one priority is, and always will be, you. When you're in a position to help someone who you see needs it, by all means, do so! But be careful not to become an enabler, doing for others what they should be doing on their own. Never give more effort to help another person than that person is giving to help himself. If he is giving a level 50 effort, your effort should never surpass 49. If he is giving an 8, you don't go past 7. If he gives a 90, you're capped at 89.

When I came home from college with professional basketball dreams, there was no one working for my future other than me. No one calling agents or teams on my behalf. No one was scouring the Internet looking for tryouts or camps I could attend. No one offering to pay for exposure-camp fees, travel, hotels, or food. I was 100 percent on my own. If anything were to happen, it would be 100 percent because of me. If nothing happened, it would be 100 percent because of me.

The people who attract the most help are the people who are helping themselves the most. They're already making things happen. Your help is like pushing a car that's already moving. It would still go forward without you.

Helping a lazy person will make him fall even harder, thanks to you. Helping someone who is not helping himself puts a person on a pedestal that he isn't prepared to stand on. When he falls—and he *will* fall—it's that much farther and harder, because someone helped more than he or she should have. Would you be proud of yourself?

When someone is given something he did not earn, he's not only ill deserving of the position, but ill equipped to handle challenges that come with it.

Let them fall on their face *now* so they don't have to fall later. If you are helping someone who isn't doing much to help herself, the best you can do is let go. Let go of your obligation to help someone succeed who does not feel obligated to go get it. Let go of your need to save the day for someone who will not save herself.

Let go of their hand. Let them walk, crawl, stand there looking stupid, or fall flat on their face. They will learn to get up and keep moving, or they won't. Either way, it is not your business. It's not your life.

• • •

What can you do when you feel you've taken action for yourself, but you could still use some guidance? How do you go about finding people who can help you, and how do you pay them back? I cover that in the next chapter, on finding and keeping mentors.

10

·————————·

MENTORSHIP

A mentor is a person who has seen what you want to see, done what you want to do, and become the person you aim to become in at least some areas of your life. While you can find success without a mentor, having one is an invaluable way to learn from someone who knows what you don't and has seen what you haven't. A person like this can save you the time, energy, money, and frustration you might have spent figuring things out on your own. You can learn from a mentor's mistakes and his or her successes—and have someone rooting for you when you need it most.

▬ MY FIRST MENTOR FOR PUBLIC SPEAKING ▬

When I first met Dawnna (whom I first mentioned in Chapter 7), I asked her why she had been willing to offer me so much of what she knew. She didn't know me, or the person who had connected us. Dawnna replied that people had shared knowledge with her at one time. She saw sharing with me as a way to pay that forward.

I wasn't the first person to ask Dawnna for help; among speakers, she was already well known. With me, however, Dawnna's advice was put to immediate use. Seeing her advice put to good use was valuable to Dawnna. It showed her that what she knew *did* work, if someone was *willing to* work. She had shared her knowledge with many people who had done nothing with it. From my own experience in sharing information with people, I wasn't surprised; this is what many people do. It's how a person can seem to know so much, yet do so little.

To this day, I am happy to call Dawnna a friend. She was as happy for and proud of me as anyone when I told her about this book. Thank you, Dawnna!

KNOW THE DIFFERENCE BETWEEN A MENTOR AND A COACH

Having a mentor is a great help. A mentor is a person who knows what you need to know, has been where you want to go, can do what you want to do, and is willing to share his or her knowledge and experience with you. There's immense value in having someone (or several people) whom you can reach with questions or challenges that they would be happy to help with.

A mentor should not be confused with a coach. A coach is hired to push and prod you to do what you need to do. A mentor is more hands-off: a mentor will share information about what works, and you can do that, or not. With the Internet, a virtual mentor can share a message one time that reaches millions of people.

Let's dig into how to find, utilize, and keep mentors, both personal and virtual, the right way.

■SUCCESSFUL PEOPLE ARE ALWAYS WILLING■ TO SHARE HOW THEY SUCCEEDED

Maybe finding a mentor has been a challenge for you. Don't be daunted: there are plenty of successful people out there who are willing to share—you just have to do the work to find them. The first step in finding a mentor is to figure out exactly what you want to learn and/or what specific area you wish to develop. Then look for people who are known and/or accomplished in that field. Tim Ferriss, author of *The 4-Hour Workweek*, advocates looking for the person who was at the top of the field 10 or 20 years ago, because this person will have the knowledge and the time because he or she is out of the spotlight and won't be so inundated with requests.

To find mentors, ask yourself the following questions:

- *Who has written books on the subject?* (Experts *always* write books!)
- *Who has a proven track record of results?*
- *Who has the most free content online?* (People who know very little probably cannot publish much material, because they would run out of knowledge at some point.)
- *Who is blogging on the topic?*
- *Who has the most fans?*
- *Whom do I best relate to?*
- *Whose background and experience is most similar to mine?*
- *Who's hitting on the exact challenges I'm experiencing right now?*

Find a person who hits even one of these, and you have a warm lead.

People who succeed are happy to tell you about themselves, what they do, and how they did it. While you may not be able to always reach someone directly and get his or her time, you can always read and learn from the content the person produces. Watch, listen, and read anything and everything people share, and you'll find that you can learn a ton—without the one-on-one conversations. I am often asked, *What would you tell your younger self?* The answer doesn't matter, because I can't speak to my younger self. But I can speak to *you* and pass along everything I wish I'd known earlier in my career. Realize that when your mentors speak, they are answering that younger-self question. They're telling you everything they wish they had known ten years, six weeks, or two hours ago. You are the "younger self" whom your mentor can't go back and talk to.

▬▬▬ DO THINGS FOR YOURSELF FIRST ▬▬▬ BEFORE YOU SEEK MENTORS

Many athletes have come to me over the years seeking mentorship that they honestly didn't even need (at least not yet). A mentor is the person you seek out after you've first taken all the action you can take yourself, and exhausted your own knowledge.

The biggest mentor-seeking mistake is expecting a mentor to do work for you that you should be doing yourself. A mentor is not there to tell you what you could have found from spending 10 minutes on Google. A mentor provides situation-specific insights *based on the actions you're taking*.

When I reached out to Dawnna, her first question was if I had any type of online presence and if I'd been doing anything for myself up to that point. Had I not had an answer to those questions, I doubt she would have been willing to give of her time.

Another mistake when people are looking for mentors is thinking that you need expert advice before you even get started on your journey. For example, this is the basketball player who says he knows he can be great if someone would just train him every day for free. Or the players who want to play overseas and want me to get them on a team. I don't give these people the time of day.

Instead, consider these practical suggestions for helping yourself:

- If you want to publish videos, turn your camera on and start recording.
- If you want to be a writer, start writing, and write every day for a year.
- If you want to be a consultant, offer your services to potential clients.
- If you have created a product, ask people to buy it!
- If you want to get better, practice.

Yes, you will probably suck at first. Maybe you'll feel embarrassed. You'll compare yourself to other, more polished people and feel you could never get to where they are. You'll realize that you have a long way to go. But the truth is, no one knows you anyway. There's no reason to feel embarrassed. And none of these reasons require the help of a mentor.

People like to join winning teams. For you, a "winning team" is a person who's taking initiative and producing some type of result. For example, had I done nothing toward my speaker ambitions before I met Dawnna, she might not have given me the time of day. But I had an established name (albeit in a completely different space), a personal brand, and online presence. I was *credible*, not just another person merely talking about doing stuff. I had proof that I was actually doing it.

People don't like to fight losing battles. Trying to help someone who's doing nothing may be a losing battle. Helping someone who is already active has a higher win probability. I once heard someone call the business world a "bandwagon industry," because once someone has some momentum, everyone else comes running after the wagon so as not to miss the ride. No one runs after a parked vehicle.

EXAMINE YOUR GAME

Take the initiative and get yourself moving;
it will be much easier to attract help.

You don't need a mentor to start doing the work. If just getting started is a real challenge for you, pay a coach who will keep a foot in your behind. That is not the job of a mentor.

A mentor is not there to do the work for you, nor should you expect your mentor to check on whether or not you're doing the work. A mentor's purpose is to help you do the right work and do it more efficiently. You will do 100 percent of the lifting. If you need help with that, again, hire a coach (this is not to say that coaches don't serve other purposes as well).

LOOK FOR SOMEONE WHO WILL TELL YOU LIKE IT IS

The amateurs and would-be pros deal with the same coaches as the eventual pros. The pros take the yelling, criticism, and incessant "you-can-do-better" prodding and keep going.

In all my years as a pro, I never once had a trainer tell me how good I was or praise my skill level. Instead, they always pushed me to play harder, run faster, and jump higher. They knew that was the only way I'd be able to hold my own against a player with equal talent.

Maybe you have or had a mentor who does the same. Someone who tells you what you need to hear in order to *get* better, not what you want to hear to *feel* better. These days, there are plenty of available mentors—and they don't have to agree to be your mentor for you to learn from them. You decide who you want to learn from, and absorb all you can from that person (so choose someone who has created, published, and shared a lot on your subject of interest).

The key step in finding a person who will tell you what you need to work on is finding someone who is not invested in your feelings. If you don't have non-BS people in your life, I suggest you start looking for them now. My podcast is a great way to get this dose of reality daily. Since we have the vastness of the Internet now, the challenge is not in finding an available mentor—it's in deciding who it will be for you (which to me is a better problem to have).

Start looking for people whose stories inspire you. Who has been where you want to go? Who embodies the type of person you aim to become in some way? Whose message seems to always hit home with you, as if she's reading your mind and knows exactly what you need to hear? Those are your mentors. Once you've found them, devour everything you can that they produce and don't stop until you're done. Then, move onto the next.

SALES 101: OFFER SOMETHING OF VALUE IN EXCHANGE FOR HELP FROM A MENTOR

Usually when we think of "offering value," we think of money. But there are many ways to offer value outside of money. Look at your life and ask yourself, is there anything you need or want that does not involve money? Of course there is. Other people, even those who are far ahead of you professionally, have their own nonmonetary needs.

Here are some of the most common nonmonetary needs people have, regardless of their title or physical resources:

- Status
- Attention
- Appreciation
- Love/connection
- Fun/variety
- Growth
- Pride
- Confidence
- Feeling of contribution
- Power

All people have needs that go beyond money. When you have a mentor, apply every piece of advice you're given as quickly as possible. This will help you, of course. It also helps your mentor in several ways:

1. When you achieve results, it shows your mentor that his or her advice is sound (which returns to your mentor status, a feeling of contribution, and power).

2. Your mentor knows his or her investment in you is time well spent (which returns to your mentor appreciation and growth).

3. As you grow in success, your mentor knows he or she played a role in that success (which returns to your mentor pride, confidence, contribution, appreciation, and power). Most of the people who've been helped by me didn't pay me directly for what they got from me. But knowing that I contributed in a small way to their success is much more valuable.

WHEN YOUR MENTOR GIVES ADVICE, FOLLOW IT!

According to Dawnna, almost all the people who had previously come to her suffered from the same afflictions. First, they were surprised that there was actual *work* involved. Second, they were unwilling to do the work.

I've been a mentor to several people over the years who grew up with my material. Many of them fell by the wayside for the same reason: the unexpected amount of work involved. No matter what profession or business, there is no hack for consistent, disciplined hard work. I'm sure a scientist in a lab somewhere is cooking up the formula to completely eliminate effort as a necessary element of success. But the potion is not ready yet. For now, you're stuck with working.

Your mentor will tell you things to do, offer suggestions, and share advice. Apply it quickly. If you're taking it in but not applying what you hear, you'll lose your mentor. Or, more accurately, your mentor will lose you.

• • •

If you're going to make an impact on the world, you will deal with other people. Whether you're selling to them, helping them, being helped, or moving them out of your way, the better you are at dealing with people, the better you'll be as a person.

In the next chapter, I'll identify and help extinguish the worst mental errors we make and show you how to avoid and overcome them.

11

BAD MENTAL ERRORS THAT GOOD PEOPLE MAKE

n my many years hearing about and helping people deal with their mental game issues, there are 12 common mistakes I see. These can happen to anyone, whether you are a good or bad person, but preventing them will transform your success. Let's take a deep dive into each and learn how to avoid and fix these mistakes in your own life.

▬▬MISTAKE #1: REPLAYING BAD MOVIES▬▬

You've seen your share of bad movies. The comedy that wasn't funny. The boring action film. The star-studded blockbuster that fell way short of the hype. Would you go to a theater and pay to see that bad movie again? Would you save it in your Netflix queue? Would you view it again even for free? Probably not. We don't want to see a bad movie twice. We erase it from memory, tell our friends how terrible it was, and try to save anyone else from suffering through it.

Yet every day, people replay the bad movies from their own lives. They mentally revisit bad situations and feel those negative feelings over and over again. Have you had your trust violated? Had your heart broken? Been promised something that wasn't delivered? Ever had a bad day, bad week, or bad year?

Athletes have bad games. My eleventh-grade basketball tryout was the worst of my three failed attempts, as a bigger, stronger player who was a grade above me overpowered and scored on me over and over again. I replayed that bad movie in my mind for weeks while I contemplated whether basketball would even be part of my future. It wasn't just one day that made this happen, either, it was the accumulation of failed attempts at erasing this bad movie and replacing it with some good memories.

Salespeople screw up presentations and talk themselves out of closes. Good people have been unjustly fired from jobs. Unpleasant stuff happens, and we can't make it un-happen. We can assess and learn from it, move on and forget about it, or drop it completely and choose to be unaffected by it. These choices are always available.

But often, people choose instead to replay those bad movies. Their unpleasant memories become feature films. If tickets were being sold, these films would break box-office records. People even invite their friends to the bad shows, sharing all the calamities they've been through with whoever will listen.

When you have a bad movie in your possession, delete the file. Remove it from your watch queue. Take it back and get a refund.

You wouldn't pay to see a bad movie twice.
So stop making the same mistakes over and over
again and go make some better movies.

MISTAKE #2: BEING TOO SMART FOR THE BASICS

Let me lay out the keys to success as briefly as possible:

1. Know what you want.
2. Make a decision to get it.
3. Know as much as you need to know about your chosen outcome.
4. Believe in yourself.
5. Work hard.
6. Keep trying until something works.
7. Once you begin achieving success, share these steps with as many people as possible.

Many educated people think they're too damn smart for the basics to apply to them. Many believe there *must* be more to success than just the simple stuff. *That's it?! There must be more to it than this basic stuff,* they say. *I already know all of that.* So experts write 250-page books to satisfy your intellect while the keys to winning never change.

Every profession, sport, or hobby has basic skill requirements. Basketball players spend whole days doing the same dribbling drills, shooting the same shots from the same spots, the same footwork, the same finishes. Is it boring, at times?

Hell, yes! Do they do it anyway? You don't become a pro if you don't do them.

To be one of the best, or get paid like it,
you need more than *knowing* the basics.
You must master their application.

Those basics are the foundation of professional careers. The fundamental skills developed in hammering on the basics are responsible for a majority of your production at work.

In business, following basic principles is how companies reach profitability and exceed expectations. It's when they get fancy, forgetting what got them there, that companies falter.

In sports, the fancy stuff you see in highlight videos makes up very little of the actual production in the real games. Watch a full basketball game and count the plays that are worthy of the highlight reel, compared to the nonhighlighted, basic stuff. But because the highlights stand out, some developing players never emphasize the basics. They learn their mistakes when they get to a level where talent alone isn't enough, and their loose grip of the basics costs them an opportunity.

In business, one of your basics may be keeping up with your paperwork and accounting for your daily disciplines. In management, you make sure people stick to and follow procedures, even though cutting corners would be easier. How much you stick to the script can often be the difference between a thriving business and a closed business.

In a 50-story high-rise building, the furnished apartments, fancy offices, and five-star restaurants may draw all the attention. However, it's the foundation of the building, buried underground and out of sight, that everything else is built on. The restaurant can be closed, gutted out, and converted to a gym. Office spaces and apartments change owners and occupants. But the foundation stays the same. The foundation is to that building what the basics are to your life, in and out of work.

▬▬▬ MISTAKE #3: HUSTLING BACKWARDS ▬▬▬

Anytime I've heard someone mention "knowing their worth," the person is referring to receiving: What they've been given or offered isn't enough. Someone offered $10; they feel they deserve $20. But the same people forget what their worth is when it comes to investing in themselves. Then, things start to cost too much or may not be worth the price.

I've never heard anyone announce that they are worth *less* than what they're given. But when it's time to give, invest, or pay up front for a later result, the same people become cost conscious and super-particular. Some even demand guaranteed results, assurances, and hard proof before committing to action.

This practice is what I call Hustling Backwards.

You're working on your game, but it's the wrong game. To conserve resources, minimize waste, and get a maximum return isn't wrong in itself. But the same way you need good defense, not just offense, to win at basketball, you have to play both sides of the game in life. If your value is high when it's time to receive, remember that value when it's time to invest in yourself.

Look at investment in yourself as an interest-bearing savings account. Basically, the more you put into that account, the more you'll have in the future, plus extra. And remember that investing in yourself is more than just money. Here are the five forms of investment:

- **Time.** This is the only element in life that you cannot survive running out of. Anything you're good at is because you have invested time. Anything worth having takes time to acquire.
- **Money.** There's no such thing as a free lunch. Your bed, electricity, toothpaste, and dinner all cost money.
- **Attention.** There's too much around for any of us to see everything. So what are you looking for? What are you noticing?
- **Focus.** The center of your attention. Humans can only focus on one thing at a time—of all the stuff that has your attention, what will you zero in on?
- **Energy.** Nothing happens without effort.

MISTAKE #4: STRUGGLING FOR MEDIOCRITY WHERE YOU DON'T BELONG

Baseball was my first official team sport, starting at age 9. At age 14, I realized I was terrible at baseball and went to basketball. I had some built-in advantages in basketball. I'm six-foot-four, not super-tall, but I was taller than most kids my age. I had long arms. I was athletic: a pretty fast runner and could jump high.

I don't know why I played baseball for so long. Probably because my father was coaching and many of my friends played baseball. Maybe I wanted to prove to myself and others that I was capable in baseball. These reasons aren't bad, but they're not good either. Most important, I was not good at baseball. The only part of baseball that came naturally was running. I could have played football, soccer, or joined a track team if running was my skill. I never experienced any successes in baseball that would have planted seeds of a future in the game.

Luckily for me, I came to this realization when I was only 14 years old. Many adults struggle with mediocrity for much longer than I did—adults who don't have even one good reason for why they're doing what they're doing. They do have plenty of bad reasons, though.

Here are all the bad reasons, followed by why you don't need to hold onto them any longer.

"This is what I've always done." This is the exact reason why you need to stop doing it! The world changes, times change, people change, information changes, and you've changed. If you are doing the same thing you've always done, you're standing still as the world moves, losing the race.

"All my friends are doing it/everyone I know is doing this." It can be hard to leave friends behind. If they're real friends, though, they'll still be friends when your paths diverge. In my senior year of college, I wasn't on the basketball team, while all my friends were. We did not become estranged; we still talk daily to this day. As of this writing, I live in Miami, while some of my closest friends live in the Northeast and West Coast of the United States.

You don't need to be doing the same thing or be in the same place for friends to remain friends. We have phones, Wi-Fi, and data plans these days. And if you lose some friends, there are 7 billion other people out there to choose from.

"I'm not a quitter." So many people trap themselves—in relationships, in careers, and anywhere else they don't want to be—with this one. There's a difference between *quitting in weakness* and *walking away in strength*.

The weakling quits when things don't go his way, someone says something he didn't like, or he's not disciplined in following a process. The person who walks away in strength has given her best effort, yet can see she's in the wrong place. Maybe there's a better idea in mind, maybe not, but she knows for sure it's not this one. If something is clearly not for you, it's your responsibility to walk away from it. There's no moral victory in remaining there when the signs are obvious.

"_____ did it/is doing it." You're not that person. What you do and what you can do has nothing to do with him or her.

"I know I can do it, I just need to _____ (take action that you could have taken a long time ago)." Everyone could _____ (achievement) if they only _____ (action). I could have been good at baseball if I could have just hit, fielded, and thrown better. I could have done better in school if I had just cared more about my grades. This faulty reasoning gets the story backward. The truth is, you *would* do better if you cared more to begin with. This doesn't mean you need to force yourself to care now. Your not caring shows that you don't belong there.

If you're struggling to just become and remain OK at what you do, know this: the world doesn't pay for mediocre. The people you know, follow, and patronize have your attention because they do something really well. If they weren't good, you wouldn't pay attention, wouldn't care, and definitely wouldn't pay for it.

• • •

But, you may be asking, what's the difference between struggling at something you could become great at and struggling at something you don't belong in? I, for example, struggled with basketball just as I had with baseball. How would one know the difference between the two? Here are four ways to tell:

1. *Do you have a future vision in it?* I could see myself getting better at basketball and becoming a top player. In baseball, all I could see was that current day.

2. *Is the struggle still fun or motivating?* I had a lot of rough days with basketball. But once I got past the emotion, I was driven all over again to get back to working on my game. After the rough days in baseball, all I saw was a dead end.

3. *Do you have any natural abilities for it?* I told you about my basketball advantages. Some baseball talents may be a strong throwing arm, and it would probably be good to not be afraid of the ball. I was a no on both.

4. *Can you feel yourself improving over time, or are you stuck in the mud?* Even as I struggled, I was getting better at basketball. I would find myself doing stuff in games that I had been practicing. I could have told you, one month after the next, how I had gotten better. In baseball, I was stagnant. I was getting older and taller, but not better.

EXAMINE YOUR GAME

Ask yourself what success means to you. Then ask yourself if continuing to struggle at what you've been working on is your best possible path for getting there. If your answer is not an immediate and definitive YES, you may be in the wrong place.

MISTAKE #5: FOCUSING TOO MUCH ON *DOING*, NOT ENOUGH ON *BEING*

In one of Napoleon Hill's lectures, he tells a story about his business partner W. Clement Stone. Stone was known as the best business-man in his town and had strong influence. A young insurance salesperson once called on Mr. Stone for help. The salesman was having trouble closing business. The salesman asked if Mr. Stone would recommend 10 prospects to call on. He asked for permission to mention Mr. Stone's name as a reference when calling on the prospects. Mr. Stone agreed, and he had 10 names and phone numbers ready for the salesman to pick up the next morning.

A week later, the young salesperson rushed back into Mr. Stone's office with exciting news. While he had previously been closing only one or two out of every 10 presentations, the sales-man had closed 8 of the prospects given to him by Mr. Stone. And he still had one more call to make later that day. This was an amazing turnaround.

The excited salesman asked if Mr. Stone would be kind enough to give him 10 *more* names to call on. Mr. Stone was busy, but he told the salesman he could use the local phone book to grab 10 more names; that's where the first 10 had come from, anyway. It took some convincing, but eventually Mr. Stone assured the young salesman that Stone had indeed grabbed 10 names and numbers randomly from the local phone book.

What changed for the salesman with those first 10, unknow-ingly random prospects, compared to his previous results? He had the same sales skills, and he was offering the same product. The only change was in his mental attitude. He was calling on people he thought had been recommended by Mr. Stone; thus his expectation and energy were different. His belief, in himself and in his product, increased.

The salesman already knew what to do. All that changed was who he was being while doing it.

Knowing that we can't get something for nothing in life, most goal-setting people want to jump right in and start taking action—which seems to be the smart thing to do. Given that this book is called *Work On Your Game*, the work part would be a good place to start, right?

Wrong.

Many people jump into doing—the physical game—without getting their mental game in order first. They may find themselves having done all the right things, yet not having the outcome they wanted. This is where people say that a technique, strategy, method, or program "doesn't work."

Let's say I gave you a recipe for baking a cake. You can put all the ingredients together correctly, but without the cake pan—the vessel—all you'll have in your kitchen is a big mess. Remember the Be-Do-Have principle I introduced in Chapter 3? The *Be* is defined as "having the state, quality, identity, nature, or role."

EXAMINE YOUR GAME

Before you take actions, check your mental state, your energy, and your focus. When the *being* is aligned, the *doing* takes care of itself.

Don't Give in to Self-Consciousness

Self-consciousness is selfish. You're in a state where you're only thinking of yourself. You give off no energy, and thus you cannot receive energy. Self-consciousness is not just a personal issue, it's an interpersonal problem. Your inability to focus on and provide value to others (which is the only way to make money or get ahead in this world, by the way) will not win friends or influence people.

Forget about yourself. You're reading this book and applying what you've read. You're taken care of. Focus on how you can give maximum value others. Doing so, you'll receive so much that you won't know what to do with it all.

MISTAKE #6: OVERTHINKING YOUR PERFORMANCE

I read an interview with actor Idris Elba, who many believe should have been named *People* magazine's "2017 Sexiest Man Alive."* Idris was asked about his style in approaching women in public. Idris advised men to immediately walk up and say something. If a man takes too long to approach, Idris advised, he ruins the moment, and maybe his golden opportunity. The longer a man takes to think about what to do or say or how, the more he psyches himself out of his chance.

Here's how to position yourself to not need to think when it's time to perform.

Prepare Your Ass Off

Be so prepared *before* the performance that everything happens exactly as it should. Work on your game so much that you can see your performance and outcome before it happens. Know

---

* Elyse Wanshel, "People on Twitter Pretty Sure Idris Elba Was Robbed of 'Sexiest Man Alive' Title," *Huffington Post*, November 15, 2017, https://www.huffingtonpost.com/entry /idris-elba-sexiest-man-alive-twitter_us_5a0ca100e4b0b37054f41977

what questions you will be asked. Be ready to handle objections. Believe so much in your preparation and performance that your energy overwhelms doubt. Nothing can throw you off, and nothing surprises you.

Visualize Your Success

On the court at my first basketball exposure camp, I started off playing too tentatively. During a time-out, I reminded myself what was on the line for my life and career. I knew my best skill was athleticism, and that using it would make me stand out. I decided then to start playing the way that would make me stand out: assertively and aggressively. I would attack the basket and try to get some dunks: people always remember dunks. Whatever happened, good or bad, would happen.

The next time I got the ball, I attacked the basket hard, drawing oohs and aahs from the crowd. That was all I needed. I made more above-the-rim plays through that weekend. The postcamp scouting report described me as an "explosive athlete" who "will dunk in traffic."

I already knew I had it, I just needed to give myself the vision.

The scouting report, along with the footage from the games, was what I used to contact agents, and one of them resulted in me signing with his agency—and led to my first professional playing job in Kaunas, Lithuania.

Our minds respond to images, not words. This is why great musicians and speakers are said to *paint pictures with their words*. It's why people make vision boards. Picture what you want in your mind, literally.

A note about visualization: visualizing success preperformance is easy when you know you've earned it. When you've done the work and positioned yourself for success before the moment, your mind is primed to deliver the corresponding vision. Without the work, you'll draw a blank.

We all have our zone, the place you can go mentally where you can perform without thinking at all. Time slows down and nothing can disturb your rhythm. Some call this a state of "flow." In the movie *The Social Network*, about the creation of Facebook, the program coders would be in their zones while writing code.

You need to know what your zone is and what gets you there. As an athlete and even now as a speaker, I find my zone by being by myself, quietly visualizing my performance. Some people get hyped up and excited. Some get a pep talk from a coach or friend. I've had teammates who would lift weights or run on cardio equipment to get into their zone. If it works for you, do it!

Practice getting in your zone so you have it on call when you need it. Michael Jordan admitted that during his first basketball hiatus, he had lost his ability to get into his zone. He spent an off-season retraining his game and his mind. The Chicago Bulls went on to win the next three NBA championships.

No matter your work, the last thing you need to do when it's game time is thinking. You're there playing, leading, presenting, or interviewing for good reason: you earned your spot. Be ready, train yourself to quiet your mind, and you won't need to think about whether you'll deliver.

MISTAKE #7: PUTTING UP INVISIBLE BARRIERS

An electric fence is a great example of an invisible barrier. I've seen its effect on a dog. After a few days of receiving a light electric shock when getting too close to the perimeter of the underground "fence" (through a device connected to a dog collar), the dog won't go anywhere near that fence. Even with the fence deactivated, the dog stays within its perimeter. This held true even when the dog was enticed with food, the call of its owner, or its favorite toy.

Humans are more complex than dogs. But we still live within our own electric fences, our invisible barriers holding us back. Use the following questions to check yourself for invisible barriers, and learn how to break them down.

1. *What ideas have you accepted from people who don't live your picture of success?* When it came to money, as a kid, I heard things like *we can't afford it*, *money doesn't grow on trees*, and *we're not rich*. All of this communicated that money existed in limited quantities that were somehow unavailable to me. Many years later, I learned otherwise.

You also may have been subjected to ideas, beliefs, and "rules" coming from authority figures in your life—people like your teachers, parents, and elder family members. Now you're old enough to examine what you were taught. You can question whether the source of the idea had what you wanted for your life or not.

Cold, harsh truth can be uncomfortable. Especially when that truth goes against our self-image. Rarely will you hear people openly admit to giving up on themselves. We rationalize it—make up a comforting story—to help ourselves feel better. People who habitually rationalize come to believe their made-up stories are true. Train yourself to be as discerning as possible when these people share ideas:

What do you see in and around this person? Does he or she have the success that you want? Has this person achieved something you aim to achieve? Has this person been where you want to go?

If you can't answer yes to any of these, you're allowing the construction of an invisible barrier around your life.

2. *What limiting beliefs are holding you back?* I refused to play basketball or do any exercise on concrete surfaces for all my years as a pro athlete. I was convinced that any high-impact activity done on the unforgiving concrete would destroy my knees. I never ran more than four miles for distance, believing any more running than that would wither away my muscle.

Then, when I was done playing basketball in 2015, I decided to try running. I hoped running would get my adrenaline pumping, and maybe replace the mental high I had obtained playing basketball. I got pretty good at the four-to-five-mile range quickly, though: basketball players normally run this distance in games, so I needed more of a challenge. I went up to running six, seven, and even eight miles. I ran multiple times per week and was shocked that my knees felt completely fine. My knees felt better when I was running than they'd felt when I'd been playing basketball. It was *basketball*, with all its jumps, changes of direction, contact, and lateral movements, that beat up my knees and ankles, not the concrete. I fell in love with running so much that I twice ran the Miami Marathon, 26.2 miles each, on concrete.

I've maintained an affinity for weight lifting after being introduced to it as a college sophomore. In my years playing in college and pro basketball, I had many teammates who avoided the weight room at all costs. The common excuse was that lifting weights would "mess up their shot." Supposedly due to the extra muscle acquired from lifting, the player would lose their shooting or dribbling skill. I always found this reasoning to be absurd. It's no different than the woman who hires a trainer and preemptively warns that she doesn't want to be "one of those big, bodybuilder women who looks like a man."

My response to the excuse-making basketball player and the fearful woman at the gym was the same. *Hello? You haven't lifted a single weight, and you're concerned with having* too much *muscle?* I've heard hundreds of people use this excuse—"I don't want to get too much of a result"—as an excuse for not starting. Too much confidence. Too much money. Too much muscle.

3. *What are you not doing because of who you think you're not?* I entered the business world with the limiting belief that a former basketball player was not "professional" enough for the business world (and wasted a lot of time trying to create a more "acceptable" image). An invisible barrier that we all face is any idea of who we are not. We convince ourselves of what we are incapable of and what we cannot achieve. All the while, we can plainly see others living the life we tell ourselves we can't.

Do they have a tool that you don't have or cannot acquire?

Do they have physical capabilities that you don't have and cannot get?

What makes them worthy of achievement, and you unworthy?

The answers are all the same: none, and nothing.

Solution: Despite being the smartest of all animals, humans are often blind to the intangibles that block us from being who we want and need to be. Be vigilant, constantly checking yourself for the invisible barriers keeping you from your destiny.

MISTAKE #8: GIVING TIME AND ATTENTION TO FEAR

Fear is caused by the belief that something or someone is dangerous. Fear feeds on two ingredients: time and attention. Many people believe we create our lives based on our thoughts and focus. Focus on good things, get good results. Do you agree? By the same token then, a focus on fear and unpleasantness creates exactly what they focus on.

Observe the sun's light shining through a magnifying glass. The magnifying glass creates a super-hot light that can start a fire. Your focus is the same, with all your resources concentrated on one task, idea, or outcome. When you're fearful and give attention to the fear, the fear grows bigger, stronger, and more formidable.

Fear grows when fed with time. When you experience fear, the worst thing you can do is hesitate, retreat, or otherwise give time to the fear—which is exactly what many people do. They put their fear on steroids, focusing on the fear, while doing nothing to address it. They talk about it, think about all the bad things that could happen, and worry about worst-case scenarios. Fearful people stop everything they're doing because fear usurps their attention. They dwell in anxiety and can't sleep, thinking about how afraid they are.

Solution: Instead, focus on the next action you *can* take, and take that action as soon as possible.

Fear Addiction

Some people are addicted to fear. They succumb to their fear of growth, expansion, and improvement rather than actually growing, expanding, or improving. But why would anyone do that? Why would someone intentionally give in to the fear?

Three reasons:

1. **Growth is inconvenient and uncomfortable.** Growth doesn't happen on our schedules.
2. **Improving means leaving behind the current you,** mentally and/or physically. Being creatures of habit, it's uncomfortable to leave familiar surroundings and touch the unknown. This can be highly stressful.
3. **The price must be paid up front with no guarantee of a return.** We like stuff that we can predict and control. Fear takes over when we're faced with taking action with no guarantee of result. The fear pushes people to retreat and never improve.

Are *you* addicted to fear? Here are four ways to know.

Your first thought is of what could go wrong. When presented with a new opportunity, what is your first thought?

- Do you think of possibilities of growth, expansion, and success?
- Do you think of the people you could help, inspire, and motivate?

Or:

- Do you think of everything that could go wrong?
- Do you dwell on the reasons why this would be a waste of time?
- Do you think about the people who tried unsuccessfully before?
- Do you think how easy it would be to stay where you are and not risk it?

Thought is free and, on a basic level, thinking about something one time has no dire consequence. Try something new and look at how things could go *right*. Look for the ways you could benefit from what you're considering. Think of how you could recover if things don't go right. Remember that imagination works both ways, and try the less-used option.

You allow failures to plant seeds of doubt. Not everyone wants to be successful. Harsh as it sounds, it's true. Many people have no goals. There are lots who tried something once, failed, and vowed to never try again. These people can preach only what they know. Listen too closely for too long, and they will plant their seeds of doubt in your mind.

Look at the people you spend the most time with:

- What do you talk about?
- Do you talk about possibilities, success, expanding, and growing?
- Are you talking about why things won't work out?
- Do you talk about how you can't see yourself successful, or why trying is a waste of time?

If you're spending time listening to people who are going backward, away from personal growth, you may be addicted to fear.

Find mentors, virtual or in-person, who plant seeds of growth. Humans are social beings. People who do positive things encourage others to do positive things. It creates company, and a pride and ego boost, too. Identify people who have what you want to have and who are who you want to be. Stick around them long enough and watch the seeds of success sprout.

You compare yourself to the average even though you're not that. In a room full of people, ask, *Who here considers himself to be average?* More than likely, no response. But, when it comes time to try something new, I'm often asked, *What results does the average person get?* Or, as someone is trying something new, they ask, *IS THIS NORMAL?* OR, *Is this how most people do it?* Few people would admit to being average, yet many people compare themselves *to* the average.

You need to decide which one is you. We all do our share of comparing:

- Are you comparing yourself to the best of the best?
- Or are you looking at "everyone" to stay close to the mean?
- Do you feel out of place doing something different from what everyone else is doing?
- Does standing out from the group make you uncomfortable?
- Do you feel your best when you are doing the same as everyone else?
- Are you *not* average, but continuously comparing yourself *to* the average?

If yes to any of the above, you may be addicted to fear.

Decide to remember that you are not like everyone else. You're an individual, and there won't be another like you, ever. Make your life a reflection of this truth. Don't compare yourself to anyone you don't want to be like.

You have the disease of indecision. You had time to think about it, consider every angle, and weigh against other options. What's stopping you from making a decision and taking action? Ask yourself these questions:

- *Am I afraid of being wrong?*
- *Do I not want the decision-making responsibility?*
- *Is it easier for me to stay in back and watch someone else take the risk?*
- *Am I resistant to change?*
- *Am I comfortable with the status quo?*

Maybe it's the action behind the decision. Taking action on a decision commits you to the decision, cutting off other possibilities. Commitment is scary to some people. If you find yourself often indecisive, you may be addicted to fear.

Solution: Understand that your best results come from actions that have your full focus. Full focus requires cutting off attention from any other consideration. Make a choice, then make that choice the best choice.

MISTAKE #9: PLACING NICENESS OVER IMPORTANCE

Someone once said, "It's nice to be important, but it's more important to be nice." Someone else repeated it. Now, millions of people live by this garbage piece of advice.

I understand the premise of the cliché. Being a good person and getting along with others is a good way to live. But this saying is a rationalization people use to feel better about their *lack* of importance.

Nice means "pleasant, agreeable, satisfactory; fine or subtle." Whereas *important* means "of great significance or value, having a profound effect on success."

It's nice to be nice, and it's important to be important. Reread those definitions above. If you had to choose only one, which would you choose to be?

We all have a basic need for significance, feeling like we matter. You wouldn't be reading a book called *Work On Your Game* if you weren't pursuing significance in some form. You don't have be aiming for worldwide fame. You become more significant with accumulated success, even when you prefer anonymity. Yet, some people have been convinced that it's more important to be nice.

Again, note that one of the synonyms for nice is *satisfactory*. In school, *satisfactory* was a grade in the "C" range. I don't want to rate any area of my life a C. I want to be on the honor roll. Consider these questions:

- *Do you want to perform to the best of your ability?*
- *Do you want to live life on the highest level?*
- *Do you believe, emotionally, that you can take your life past the satisfactory "C" level?*
- *Do you want to earn more money at your job or in your business?* What do you think will achieve it faster: being more satisfactory, or more effective on the success of the company?
- *Would you like to play more on your sports team?* What will get it for you faster, and for longer: being nice to the coach, or becoming a more important player?

If you've been on a date with a woman or man whom you described as "nice," there probably was not a second date.

When meeting with your boss, are you more concerned with being nice, or addressing the important orders of business? Which one does your boss care about?

When you read a book, do you think the author would rather this book be nice, or important? Which one do you think sells more books?

Think of the most recent nice person you met. Then think of a recent important person you met. Who do you remember better?

Being important and significant doesn't mean being a jerk or that you have no compassion for people. It doesn't mean you can't smile and say hello in the elevator. Quite the contrary. The nicest people I know, coincidentally, are also some of the most well-known, well-paid, and important people I've met.

The nastiest, rudest people who cross my path are always unimportant people. Their lack of importance causes them to seek significance in other ways, such as belittling people.

Their lack of significance gives them fewer reasons to be happy. The cycle is self-perpetuating, as their nastiness drives people away, ruining their chances of ever being important.

Personally, as my importance has grown, I've become a nicer person. I'm more secure with myself. I've built lasting relationships with important people whose niceness rubs off on me. And as I've had a more profound effect on my own success, I have more reasons to smile and be nice!

Being important doesn't mean you can't be nice. Nice and important are not mutually exclusive. The cliché tells you that a nice person should find solace in insignificance, and that an important person must be some kind of jerk.

False.

Being a pleasant and agreeable person does not mean you can't be a high-value individual who is also very successful. People of great significance and high value do pleasant things. The more important you are, the nicer you can be. Important people give to charity, donate to positive causes, and help people in need. I met an important person last week, a Hall of Fame athlete, and one of the first things she mentioned was the work her charitable foundation does. When you're important, you're in a position to be as nice as you want to be, as often as you want to be. When you're unimportant, your niceness is limited. Unimportant people may lack the resources to do nice things.

Can you do really nice things without resources like money and connections? Of course. At the same time, we can all agree that food, clothing, shelter, electricity, access, and material goods are all important. And they all require resources.

Important people make things happen.

When you are important, *of high significance and value, having a profound effect on success*, you have power. Power is influence: the ability to make things happen (or not happen) by the force of your resources. Consider these questions:

- Do you want to make things happen?
- Do you want your effect to be felt at your job, on your team, in your family, in your life?
- Do you want your name to be remembered after you're gone?
- Are there personal changes you wish to make that haven't happened yet?

If you answered yes to any of these, then making things happen is part of your plan. A significant, high-value person must make things happen to have a profound effect on success.

Nice people can be taken advantage of. Important people already have the advantage. When I needed a weekend off to attend that first basketball exposure camp, I cut a deal with my boss to get the days off, to be made up later that summer. He was willing to work with me not because I was nice, but because I made a lot of membership sales at the gym: I had a profound effect on his success as the club's manager.

In business and sports, importance beats niceness every time. Become as important as you can be, so you can afford to be nicer.

In your professional experience, you already know: satisfactory results don't cut it. For an American playing overseas basketball, satisfactory players receive coach-class flights back to the United States as soon as an important player becomes available. Important performers in any profession have more offers and choices than they can possibly fulfill.

Solution: Remember, being important does not mean not being nice. It means understanding that your profound effect on success gets you all the nice things you want, in abundance.

MISTAKE #10: DISRESPECTING YOUR SUCCESS

As you learned in Chapter 6, "Mental Toughness," success is egotistical and sensitive. Success doesn't tolerate the smallest slight, even if it's just a joke. Success will not accept being disrespected. If you've ever had some success but were unable to repeat or build upon it, you may have disrespected your success. Here's an example of how it happens:

Susie tried out for her school basketball team. She made the team, but her teammates were better players than Susie. They had more experience and skill. So Susie sat on the bench for most of the season.

The following offseason, Susie e-mailed me about her predicament. She had plans of playing in the WNBA, and her two-point-per-game freshman season wasn't good enough. Susie knew she needed to get better, but she was impatient with the process. She asked me, *Dre, how can I get much better, faster?*

Maybe you think Susie was doing nothing wrong. She was young, ambitious, and impatient to reach her goals. It's natural to want to fast-forward your success, right?

No.

Every great success must adhere to a process. The process must be followed, and above that, it must be respected. When you're among those who are better than you, know that they all followed a process to get to where they are (even if they don't know it). They just started theirs before you.

Susie's two-point-per-game freshman season was part of her process. She needed to go through it for her development. Does every player need this exact experience? Not necessarily, but there's only one Suzie. Her path is *her* path. Susie's belief that she should have been playing more and scoring more is a slap in the face to the process. Getting better is not a magic trick. Without completing the five-point investment process I described earlier in this chapter in Mistake #3 (Time-Money-Attention-Focus-Energy), Suzie has not yet paid the price to match her expectations.

Anyone who doesn't wish to follow the process isn't serious about succeeding. Anything you accomplish, no matter how small, you need to respect and treat as a building block toward what's next. When you talk down on yourself or your accomplishments, you're letting success know how little you value it. You're telling success that it's accepted only when presented a certain way as determined by you.

Solution: Celebrate, or at least appreciate, each step in your journey. It's all part of the process. Every great achievement resulted from a process that started small. *Your* success is no exception.

MISTAKE #11: WHINING

Things happen in life. Things you don't want. Things that are the exact opposite of what you want. Unexpected things. They'll cost you money, time, and other stuff you value. The worst thing you can do is bitch, whine, and complain about it when they happen.

Implant the following belief into your psyche: Things happen because of you, not to you.

If you've read my book, *The Mental Workbook*, and know how the subconscious mind works, you understand this. Your thoughts and energy always attract their kind. Therefore, everything in your life is a result of something you did or did not do. Accepting that everything happens *because* of you gives you power to create outcomes. If things just happen *to* you, you're a victim who cannot control your life. Ask yourself what you can do, not why it's so bad.

When my college basketball career abruptly ended during my junior year, that could have been a death sentence to everything basketball for me. Instead, driving back to my off-campus apartment from the gym, I started reconstructing my path and vision for how I'd become a professional player now that playing in college was no longer part of the process.

Checking for fear is our default human mindset when something happens. *Am I in danger? Could I possibly be hurt? Do I need to flee the scene?*

You've recovered from unpleasant happenings and lived to talk about them. The proof is the fact that you're alive to read this. When things turn the wrong way, ask yourself what you can do about it instead of basking in the terror. I promise, you will have answers.

Solution: Never complain, except to get charged up to create change. Whining and complaining are not in the achiever's arsenal. If you catch yourself bitching, whining, or complaining, let it be for one reason: Priming yourself to take action about the situation at hand.

MISTAKE #12: BEING A PIG: "PROFESSIONAL INFORMATION GATHERER"

I get e-mails and direct messages from people who claim they need help. Topics range from sales, the crossover dribble, self-publishing, and other how-do-I-do-this areas. This missing knowledge of how-to seems to be the only thing keeping many people from winning.

Here's the truth: information is available in such vast amounts, you're more likely to drown in it than die from a lack of it.

If a *lack of information* is the only thing keeping you from success, you're either incredibly lazy or ignoring the real issue. You probably know very well what that real issue is. I know for damn sure it's not a lack of information.

Our technologically advanced world has created a brand-new reason to delay action: gathering more information. Some people become quite proficient at this task. I call them PIGs: "Professional Information Gatherers."

How can you know if you are one? Check yourself against the following PIG symptoms.

Information Begets a Need for More of It

You can be buried alive in information. For a PIG, more information means more questions to ask, and more reasons for delay. PIGs research, gather, examine, and compare, just to make themselves more confused. PIGs asks minutiae questions that are nothing more than time-wasters. When PIGs don't get answers to their questions, they have a built-in excuse for doing nothing: *I don't know how!*

Gathering all the information you can is not a bad idea. But to insist on reviewing, organizing, and memorizing it all before doing anything else *is* a bad idea. Information is always multiplying. A PIG can find himself or herself quickly buried in information. Rolling around in dirt (that is, information) is unproductive, but PIGs enjoy it. Professional Information Gatherers swap dirt for information to keep their suits clean. When done, the PIG still has nothing to show.

As time moves forward, the stagnant PIG eventually loses the game. The PIG becomes a topping on a bacon cheeseburger, or a Christmas ham with a tomato stuffed in its mouth. They say professional sports careers are short. The PIG's time is even shorter. For more help eradicating the PIG virus, reread Chapters 7 and 8 on Personal Initiative.

• • •

The mental errors we discussed in this chapter can seep into your conditioning quietly and without you noticing. So be sure you consistently check yourself and use the provided fixes for each to keep your mind working for you and not against you.

12

DON'T LIVE BY THE BOOK

I put a lot of time and energy into this book. I believe it's a damn good book. Despite this, do not live your life strictly by my words. No speaker, author, coach, actor, athlete, or guru knows what's best for you. Aside from helping you to Work On Your Game, I don't know what's best for you. I cannot think for you. I can't make your decisions. Once decisions are made and actions are taken, I cannot live the resulting life for you.

If you read this book, take a ton of notes, then do nothing, that's on you. If you read 10 more books after this one without taking the necessary actions, that's on you.

I am your guide, your virtual coach, helping you get where you want to go. But YOU will be getting there, not me. When you win as a result of Working On Your Game, I surely want to know about it, but I won't be the reason it happened; that would be because of you. When you become who you need to be, take the actions you need to take, and life is what you've always envisioned, it will be because of you.

We don't build statues for committees or advisors, that happens only for the people who stand on the front lines and make it happen. Work hard and you can be that person.

Congratulations on the investment you've made in reading *Work On Your Game*. I wrote it with the intention of changing lives. You are the holder of your destiny.

Work On Your Game. #WOYG

INDEX

ABOUT THE AUTHOR

 **Dre Baldwin** is owner of Work On Your Game Inc. and creator of The Third Day Process of Discipline. A nine-year professional basketball player, Dre teaches professionals and athletes how to achieve results via Discipline, Confidence, Mental Toughness, and Personal Initiative.

Dre started publishing videos to YouTube in 2006, creating the athlete training video genre in the process. Since then, he has also created nearly 200 courses and programs. Dre has given 4 TEDxTalks and written 18 books. His Work On Your Game Podcast has amassed over 1.5 million listens. A Philadelphia native, Dre lives in Miami.